THE GIRL NEXT DOOR

by Alan Ayckbourn

‖SAMUEL FRENCH‖

Copyright © 2023 by Haydonning Ltd
All Rights Reserved

THE GIRL NEXT DOOR is fully protected under the copyright laws of the British Commonwealth, including Canada, the United States of America, and all other countries of the Copyright Union. All rights, including professional and amateur stage productions, recitation, lecturing, public reading, motion picture, radio broadcasting, television, online/digital production, and the rights of translation into foreign languages are strictly reserved.

ISBN 978-0-573-00024-9

concordtheatricals.co.uk
concordtheatricals.com

FOR AMATEUR PRODUCTION ENQUIRIES

United Kingdom and World
excluding North America
licensing@concordtheatricals.co.uk
020-7054-7298

Each title is subject to availability from Concord Theatricals, depending upon country of performance.

CAUTION: Professional and amateur producers are hereby warned that *THE GIRL NEXT DOOR* is subject to a licensing fee. The purchase, renting, lending or use of this book does not constitute a licence to perform this title(s), which licence must be obtained from the appropriate agent prior to any performance. Performance of this title(s) without a licence is a violation of copyright law and may subject the producer and/or presenter of such performances to penalties. Both amateurs and professionals considering a production are strongly advised to apply to the appropriate agent before starting rehearsals, advertising, or booking a theatre. A licensing fee must be paid whether the title is presented for charity or gain and whether or not admission is charged.

This work is published by Samuel French, an imprint of Concord Theatricals Ltd.

Professional Performing Rights: applications for performance by professionals in any medium and in any language throughout the world should be addressed to Casarotto Ramsay & Associates Ltd, www.casarotto.co.uk email: rights@casarotto.co.uk.

No one shall make any changes in this title for the purpose of production. No part of this book may be reproduced, stored in a retrieval system, scanned, uploaded, or transmitted in any form, by any means, now known or yet to be invented, including mechanical, electronic, digital, photocopying, recording, videotaping, or otherwise, without the prior written permission of the publisher. No one shall share this title, or part of this title, to any social media or file hosting websites.

The moral right of Alan Ayckbourn to be identified as author of this work has been asserted in accordance with Section 77 of the Copyright, Designs and Patents Act 1988.

USE OF COPYRIGHTED MUSIC

A licence issued by Concord Theatricals to perform this play does not include permission to use the incidental music specified in this publication. In the United Kingdom: Where the place of performance is already licensed by the PERFORMING RIGHT SOCIETY (PRS) a return of the music used must be made to them. If the place of performance is not so licensed then application should be made to PRS for Music (www.prsformusic.com). A separate and additional licence from PHONOGRAPHIC PERFORMANCE LTD (www.ppluk.com) may be needed whenever commercial recordings are used. Outside the United Kingdom: Please contact the appropriate music licensing authority in your territory for the rights to any incidental music.

USE OF COPYRIGHTED THIRD-PARTY MATERIALS

Licensees are solely responsible for obtaining formal written permission from copyright owners to use copyrighted third-party materials (e.g., artworks, logos) in the performance of this play and are strongly cautioned to do so. If no such permission is obtained by the licensee, then the licensee must use only original materials that the licensee owns and controls. Licensees are solely responsible and liable for clearances of all third-party copyrighted materials, and shall indemnify the copyright owners of the play(s) and their licensing agent, Concord Theatricals Ltd., against any costs, expenses, losses and liabilities arising from the use of such copyrighted third-party materials by licensees.

IMPORTANT BILLING AND CREDIT REQUIREMENTS

If you have obtained performance rights to this title, please refer to your licensing agreement for important billing and credit requirements.

THE GIRL NEXT DOOR was first produced by Stephen Joseph Theatre, Scarborough (Round auditorium), on 8th June, 2021.

Due to the original production taking place in the aftermath of the 2021 Covid-19 lockdown, the production featured two socially-bubbled companies (Red Team and Blue Team). If a member of the Red Team received a positive Covid test, then the Blue Team would take over performances. The companies were individually directed by Alan Ayckbourn (Red) and Chelsey Gillard (Blue). The Blue Team also performed in a limited number of shows within the original schedule. The cast was as follows:

Red Team

ROB (ROBERT) HATHAWAY..Bill Champion
ALEX HATHAWAY..Alexandra Mathie
ALF TINDLE..Linford Johnson
LILY TINDLE..Naomi Petersen

Blue Team

ROB (ROBERT) HATHAWAY..Michael Hobbs
ALEX HATHAWAY..Eliza McClelland
ALF TINDLE..Tayla Kovacevic-Ebong
LILY TINDLE..Georgia Burnell

Director: Alan Ayckbourn (Red Team)
Associate Director: Chelsey Gillard (Blue Team)
Design: Kevin Jenkins
Lighting: Jason Taylor
Sound: Alan Ayckbourn
Sound Associate: Paul Stear

Company Stage Manager: Fleur Hill-Beeley
Deputy Stage Manager: Sue Volans
Assistant Stage Manager: Rachel Stevens

CHARACTERS

ROB (ROBERT) HATHAWAY – Sixty, an actor
ALEX HATHAWAY – Sixty two, his sister, a government financial adviser
ALF TINDLE – Twenty six, a soldier
LILY TINDLE – Twenty four, his wife

SETTING

The partial view of adjoining terrace houses and back gardens of numbers fifteen and seventeen Maple Street, Canonbury, London N1.

TIME

The date is 5th August for both locations but for number fifteen it is 2020 whilst for number seventeen it is 1942, some seventy-eight years earlier.

ACT ONE

Scene One

(Early one fine August morning in London.)

(A composite setting comprising the partial view of two adjoining terrace houses, numbers 15 and 17 Maple Street, Canonbury, London N1. Visible are their respective back kitchens and small rear gardens with a hedge dividing them. Both gardens are in marked contrast. The garden of number 15 consists mostly of an unkempt lawn surrounded by overgrown flowerbeds. Whilst at number 17 the garden has been transformed into a rudimentary allotment.)

(The respective kitchens, too, could not be more contrasting. At number 15, home of today's modern Hathaway family, it is thoroughly modern and up to date with every labour-saving device imaginable. Whereas at number 17, the 1942 home of the Tindles, in the midst of surviving the onslaught of World War Two, it is a far more spartan affair, although scrupulously maintained.)

(At the start, **ROB**, *an actor aged sixty, casually dressed in a T-shirt and tracksuit bottoms, is sitting in his kitchen at number*

15 gazing gloomily out of the window into his back garden.)

(After a moment, next door at number 17, **LILY**, *a woman in her twenties comes out of the back door into her own garden carrying a washing basket. She goes down the path to the end and disappears out of sight.)*

*(****ROB****, catching sight of her through his window, frowns.)*

ROB. *(Muttering to himself.)* Hello. Who the hell are you, young lady? What might you be doing there, I wonder?

(He cranes his neck to watch her further without getting up.)

*(****ALEX****, his sister, a couple of years his senior, enters from the hall. She is incongruously dressed. Whilst her top half is dressed for the office, suit jacket and crisply ironed shirt, make up, jewellery, et cetera, below the waist she is still wearing her pyjama bottoms and slippers.)*

ALEX. *(As she enters.)* Sorry. Stuck upstairs in the office. These early morning zoom meetings, quite unnecessary. I don't know why she insists on holding them at the crack of dawn, we're all of us stuck at home, anyway. She could hold them any old time. Have you had any breakfast, yet?

ROB. I managed to grab a slice of cold pizza we had left over from last night.

ALEX. God, Rob! I keep telling you, you need a proper meal, darling…

ROB. Yeah, yeah, yeah! The most important meal of the day, I know. So you keep telling me every single morning.

ALEX. It's true!

ROB. And I keep telling you, these days I don't need hearty breakfasts. They're only important if I'm going somewhere to build myself up to face the day. But if the day only consists of me sitting here, bored to death staring at the same piece of wall, week in, week out, till it's supper time, I can't see what I'm supposed to be building up for... what the hell are you wearing anyway?

ALEX. I was running late this morning, got dressed in a hurry. It's alright, nobody sees your bottom half at these meetings, do they? I'm convinced half of them aren't wearing anything at all. Gives some of the junior officials some sort of vicarious thrill, sitting there half naked at a Treasury meeting with all their bits showing...

ROB. I hope you don't intend to do that...

ALEX. God, no. You've only got to nudge the web cam a fraction for all to be revealed... whoops, beg your pardon, Chancellor, you weren't meant to see that, sorry.

> *(Under the last, **ALEX** has located a bowl and spoon, together with a packet of cornflakes. In passing, she switches on the kettle to make them both tea.)*

You want some of these...?

ROB. No, thanks.

ALEX. *(Serving herself.)* You don't need to stare at a wall there, surely? I keep telling you, you need to find a nice fulfilling hobby...

ROB. Oh, right, what a good idea! I'll start a stamp collection...

ALEX. I'm sure other people in your position find plenty to do...

ROB. ...make a scale matchstick model of the House of Commons and then set fire to the bloody place...

*(During the next, **ALEX** completes preparing her cereal and proceeds to eat it.)*

ALEX. ...I mean you're not the only one, are you? You're hardly unique. There must be hundreds of actors who've suddenly found themselves out of work... I'm sure most of them don't sit and sulk all day. I'm sure most of them are finding things to do...

ROB. I hear most of them are getting extremely inventive. Shakespearean sonnets performed by glove puppets, reciting favourite soliloquies while sitting on the toilet... I'm sorry, Alex, I'm slowly going mad here. I'm just about at my wits end, I really am. Another month of not seeing another living soul...

ALEX. Well, please spare a thought for me, Rob, stuck here with you. I never chose to be here, did I? I'd far sooner be back home with Janice, I really would. I miss her terribly. Only she's got her wretched mother to cope with, of course...

ROB. ...whilst you're stuck here with your wretched brother, of course...?

ALEX. No, sorry I didn't mean it that way. But I do worry for you, really. All on your own here. Now you don't even have June to look after you. If you hadn't had that row and kicked her out –

ROB. Only after I'd been asking her for weeks in a most civilised manner to keep her squalid little extramarital affairs away from the gutter press. But, of course, she chose to stay, continuing to live off my slender earnings –

ALEX. Yes, I know, I know, I know. She behaved disgracefully. I told you, you should never have married her. She was far too young for you. She wasn't worthy of you, Rob.

ROB. The writing was on the wall wasn't it, when I even started getting letters from my fans warning me about her… "Dear Mr Hathaway, I am an old age pensioner and a long-standing fan of yours. I was so sorry to read of your wife's appalling behaviour…" I've still got that letter framed on the lavatory wall, haven't I? In all its ghastly pink paper and nauseous purple ink glory. I put it there as a reminder to my errant wife. Anyway. Water under the bridge. Divorced and gone for ever. Good riddance. *(Slight pause.)* Sorry to go on, Alex, but you have to admit I've good reason to be depressed, haven't I? Second marriage up the spout, my career's smashed into a brick wall. Now, on top of that, all this lockdown bollocks. I can't even leave the bloody house, go for a pint. Trapped…

ALEX. You're hardly unique, you know. It's the same for everyone. Mostly everyone, anyway.

> (**ALEX**, *having finished her cereal, puts the bowl and spoon into the dishwasher, already filled with the dirty dishes from the night before.*)
>
> (*During the next, she finishes making the tea.*)

ROB. At least you've still got a job. Providing you keep your knickers on…

ALEX. For the time being, anyway. I think they're soon going to start cutting back, you know…

ROB. …at least you can go upstairs and type out your reports and your projections – hold your zoom meetings… It's different for us actors – we need – human contact – fellowship. People. A bloody audience for God's sake. Just the touch of another person… Another sentient human being, you know. I might be reduced to investing in one of those sex dolls. I could order one online…

ALEX. If you do that, Rob, I promise you I'll be straight off. Lockdown or no, I refuse to share a house with you and a garish inflatable woman... can you imagine the three of us, sitting here at mealtimes trying to make small talk, her with her mouth wide open...? I'm sorry, I couldn't be doing with that...

(*ROB sits gloomily.*)

(*Studying him anxiously.*) I hope we're not about to go into one of your lows again, are we? I couldn't cope again, Rob, not after the last time.

(*A silence.*)

You barely remember, do you? It was a nightmare for the rest of us. You were in the most dreadful state – day after day, hopelessly drunk, punching your fellow actors, setting fire to valuable props, threatening that poor young producer...

ROB. (*Muttering.*) Little bastard never liked me. Right from the off. From the minute he tiptoed out of Cambridge. Precocious little shit...

ALEX. I don't know why you stayed as long as you did, quite frankly. You'd been saying for years you wanted to leave the series. (*Placing the tea beside him.*) Here you are.

ROB. Yes, but not like that! I didn't expect to leave like that! After six years of loyal service, I expected more than that. The least they could have done was to give Tiger a dignified exit. The man was a hero, for God's sake, a national hero! George Tiger Jennings. A living legend amongst fire-fighters. At least they could have arranged it so that he died, whilst single-handedly saving St Paul's Cathedral from incendiary bombs or rescuing two hundred sick kids from Great Ormond Street from a V2 rocket. Some act of gallantry worthy of a World War Two legend. But what did they dream up instead, that pack of subhuman Neanderthals? Tiger jumping off to rescue a dog from a bomb crater and being accidentally run over by his own bloody fire engine. What way is that for a hero to go?

ALEX. Oh, come on, there'll be other jobs, surely? That's what you always say, isn't it?

ROB. After years of being, as my absentee agent so tactfully puts it, 'currently unavailable', I somehow doubt it. Half the general public, the ones over fifty, the ones who can still remember, still believe I am Tiger fucking Jennings, anyway.

ALEX. Oh, by the way there was a rather nice article in the *Guardian* online this morning about heroes. I ran it off for you. *NFS* gets a mention. It's quite nice about you. Lovely photo. Hadn't seen it before. Here.

(She pushes across the piece of paper with the printed off article.)

ROB. Thanks. These you have loved, eh?

(A brief glum pause.)

ALEX. Sorry. I need to get on.

ROB. Westminster calls.

ALEX. Well, someone's got to keep the country going.

ROB. I wouldn't rely on this current mob.

ALEX. Rob, darling, do try and cheer up a little.

ROB. Yes, big sister.

ALEX. Every single morning, you're the same. Watch television or something.

ROB. *(With a sustained groan.)* Oh, God! The choice of another bloody boxset or daytime TV! Spare me!

ALEX. *(Hovering in the doorway.)* See you later. I'll check on you at lunchtime. As usual. I warn you, though, if you're still in this mood I'm going straight up again.

ROB. I meant to tell you, there was a strange woman in the next-door garden just now…

ALEX. What, the Jessops' garden?

ROB. Hanging out her washing, down at the end there…

ALEX. I thought the Jessops were in Dorset? They opted to isolate in their country place, surely? Odd. Better see who it is, I suppose. Be on the safe side. They may have let it to someone, of course…

ROB. What, those two? I can't imagine them letting their precious little show home to anyone common enough to hang out their washing, appalling pair of right-wing snobs.

ALEX. I'll give their keyholder a ring, anyway. Check they haven't let it and not told us. They left his number somewhere. A nephew. Ian – something. I think.

ROB. If I see the woman again, I'll have a word. She looked harmless enough. Fairly young –

ALEX. Yes, well, behave yourself. Remember to keep your social distance. Keep your side of the hedge.

*(**ALEX** goes out.)*

*(**ROB** studies the newspaper article.)*

ROB. Even spelt my bloody name wrong, as well. Robert Hadaway and fellow members of BBC One's popular 90s series, *NFS*.

(He tosses the paper aside.)

*(In the other garden, **LILY**, her washing basket now full of clean washing, returns towards the house.)*

*(**ROB** rises rapidly and goes through his kitchen door into his own garden. On the hopeful assumption that he will be recognised, he adopts his public persona, a mixture of easy genial charm and quiet masculine confidence.)*

(Calling as he goes.) I say! Hello! Hello there! I say.

LILY. *(Smiling.)* Oh, hello.

ROB. Can I help you?

LILY. Beg your pardon?

ROB. Can I help you at all?

LILY. No, that's very kind of you, thank you. It's not heavy, I can manage.

ROB. No, that's not quite what I –

LILY. Thank you for asking. I thought I'd better fetch it in. Just in case.

ROB. Sorry?

LILY. My washing. Just in case.

ROB. Oh, yes?

LILY. They said it might rain later. The man on the wireless. He warned us it might...

ROB. Did he now?

LILY. ...mind you, he usually gets it wrong, doesn't he? More often than not. For all we know, could be in for a heatwave, couldn't we, eh? *(She laughs.)* I'm Mrs Tindle by the way. Lily. How d'you do?

ROB. Oh, yes? Hello! I take it you're looking after the place, are you?

LILY. Beg your pardon?

ROB. I assume you're looking after the house for them? For the Jessops?

LILY. For the what?

ROB. The Jessops. While they're away? Carol and Tony Jessop. While they're in Dorset?

LILY. No, I've never heard of them. They live in Dorset, do they?

ROB. No, no, no, they live there. In that house.

LILY. What, here? At number 17? This is our house.

ROB. *(With a smile.)* With due respect, I have to tell you that we – I've lived here for nearly ten years and I've never seen you before.

LILY. With respect, we've lived here seven years, ever since we were married and I've never seen you before, neither.

ROB. *(A bit stumped.)* Yes. Well. *(He laughs.)*. Bit of an impasse, eh?

LILY. Beg your pardon?

ROB. Your move. As they say in chess. Your move. *(He laughs again.)*

LILY. I'm not moving.

ROB. You don't recognise me at all, do you?

LILY. No.

ROB. But you're thinking, aren't you, I know the face from somewhere? I definitely know his face. That's what you're thinking.

LILY. No.

ROB. Go on, have a guess, then. Who am I?

LILY. *(Hesitantly.)* I think – I think you're from next door. From Mrs Doggett's. You must be staying with

Mrs Doggett. Are you a relation of Elsie's, then – Elsie Doggett's? She never mentioned you at all.

ROB. *(Slightly taken aback.)* I take it you don't watch TV much, then?

LILY. *(Shaking her head, puzzled.)* Sorry?

ROB. Television? You're not a keen viewer, it seems?

LILY. I've no idea what you're talking about, sorry.

ROB. NFS. You must have heard of NFS? It's repeated endlessly, practically every night.

*(**LILY** looks blank.)*

NFS. National Fire Service.

LILY. *(With sudden realisation, her face brightening.)* Oh, them! You're part of them, are you? That's amazing!

ROB. Ah, you have heard of it?

LILY. Yes, of course I've heard of them! The firemen, of course I've heard of the firemen! I think they're the bravest people I know. They're my heroes! You're one of my heroes!

ROB. Oh, yes? Here we go…

LILY. Actually if you must know, all us girls round here, we have a thing about you. You know, nothing serious. You know about being rescued, and all that…

ROB. *(Who's heard it all before.)* Yeah, yeah, yeah…

LILY. …being carried down a ladder, you know…

ROB. …in your frilly nightie, yes all of that. Actually, if you want the truth, Lily – Lily, is it –?

LILY. Lily, yes…

ROB. …in actual fact, Lily, most of it's vastly exaggerated. Just for the programme. Flights of fancy by the writers – so as not to depress the viewers. In reality, it was all a damn sight grimmer. Nightmarish times, those were…

LILY. Yes, dreadful…

ROB. …over thirty-one thousand Londoners killed or seriously injured over that period…

LILY. …oh, as many as that, I'd no idea…

ROB. …three million and a quarter properties destroyed by German bombs…

LILY. … I didn't realise, they don't tell you that, do they…

ROB. …fifteen hundred fires burning in one single night, most of them out-of-control…

LILY. …that's terrible, they never tell you any of this, do they…?

ROB. I mean, let's face it, *NFS*, it's just a pre-watershed, watered down family show, isn't it? A bit of harmless entertainment. All a bit of a laugh basically, isn't it? I mean, at the end of the day, us lot from Equity, we all had a shower, quick drink in the club bar and then off home safely to our cosy little beds, didn't we?

LILY. *(Staring at him admiringly.)* You're so casual about it, aren't you? Risking your life and laughing about it like that. I just can't get over your bravery…

ROB. *(Modestly.)* Yes, well, thanks. *(Smiling.)* It takes a lot of courage, working for the Beeb, occasionally. *(He laughs.)* Seriously, Lily, all I'm saying is, it's different for us today. I mean, we continually describe these as difficult times but really and truly we should count ourselves lucky, shouldn't we?

LILY. Quite right, we should! Very lucky! Last year, it got really bad. Mind you, we're still here, aren't we? Won't let 'em get us down, will we? Not us Londoners!

ROB. Aha! That's the spirit!

(A pause. They smile at each other.)

(Slightly awkwardly.) Listen, Lily, I hate to break this up – it's been great talking to you – and so on – and – *(Laughing.)* – now you've remembered who I am – if you – want an autograph – a signed picture of Tiger perhaps – I'm happy to oblige – but the point is, I really ought to be seeing you on your way, you know. I mean frankly, by rights, you've no business being here, have you?

LILY. Oh, no! I shouldn't be here at all! Thanks for reminding me! It's my Gladys morning. It's my morning for Gladys.

ROB. Your morning for what?

LILY. Auntie Gladys. It's my morning with her. We take turns. Me and my sister-in-law, Margaret. When she's not driving her ambulance. I must be going...

ROB. *(A trifle bemused.)* Have you far to go?

LILY. No, only just round the corner. In Pelham Street. Number eleven. My parents' old house.

ROB. I see.

LILY. I wonder – I wonder if you'd mind – giving me a hand...?

ROB. Yes. Right. Ready and willing. Anything you want carrying. Happy to help. So long as we keep our distance, eh?

LILY. No, it's just the kitchen tap in there...

ROB. Kitchen tap?

LILY. ...it's stuck again, wretched thing. I can't turn it off proper. Not strong enough, I'm afraid...

ROB. *(Uncertain.)* Yes... I'll have a go for you. I'll come over there to you, shall I?

LILY. You'd better. Unless you got very long arms. *(She laughs.)*

> *(**ROB** laughs with her. He then steps through the hedge onto her side.)*

ROB. ... I think it should be safe enough...

LILY. *(As he does so.)* No, it's not dangerous, at all. It just needs a plumber. But it's impossible to get hold of one, these days.

ROB. Right. Tell me about it.

LILY. I mean, I can't even get hold of my brother William and he's qualified...

ROB. Absolute pain, isn't it, this social distancing it's – *(Noticing the garden for the first time.)* My God! What's happened here? What's all this? It's like a ploughed field.

LILY. Careful! You're standing on the beetroots.

ROB. *(Jumping aside.)* Oh, sorry.

LILY. My pride and joy, those are...

ROB. Where the roses used to... What have you done with the lawn? Where's their lawn gone?

LILY. Oh, we had to get rid of that. Dug it up last year. Took up too much growing space. Besides, we never used the grass that much. Once the children were...went away. And we all need to do our bit, don't we?

ROB. How do you mean?

LILY. These days?

ROB. Oh, I see what you mean. Food shortages, yes. Well, you know, I think that was all greatly exaggerated. Once all the panic buying died down. It doesn't seem to be too serious...

LILY. Well, it may be all right for you firemen, you probably get special rations, don't you? I should think you're taken care of because you're special, aren't you? But for the rest of us, with all this rationing, it's not easy, you know, these days, making ends meet at all. We all of us need to get our heads down, don't we? Dig for victory.

ROB. *(Uneasily.)* Dig for…? I see.

(He stares down the end of the garden.)

(Tentatively.) Tell me – Lily – I can call you Lily, may I …?

LILY. Course.

ROB. That metal – construction – at the end there – the big thing covered with earth…?

LILY. Oh, Alfie, my husband, he put that together for us before he went away.

ROB. …correct me if I'm wrong, but that's a – isn't that a –?

LILY. That's our shelter, yes.

ROB. An Anderson Shelter?

LILY. Anderson Shelter, that's right. You never seen one before? You must have done, surely? In your line, you must have done?

ROB. Oh, sure. Yes. We featured one in Season Two when I had to rescue a couple of kids who were… *(He tails off.)*

LILY. What's that? You rescued someone, did you?

ROB. Let's take a look at this tap of yours, shall we?

LILY. *(Leading him indoors.)* I'd appreciate it. Thank you so much, Mr – oh, look I never did get your name, did I? Mr –?

ROB. George. Jennings.

LILY. Do come in, Mr Jennings –

ROB. George.

LILY. George.

ROB. They tend to call me Tiger.

LILY. Tiger George. That's nice. Do come in, please...

> *(There is something clearly developing between them.)*
>
> *(**ROB** follows her in, never taking his eyes off her. She does the same.)*

You'll have to pardon the muddle, it's a bit untidy, I'm afraid. I wasn't expecting company this morning.

ROB. That's alright, I'm used to –

> *(He catches his first glimpse of the room.)*

(Softly.) Oh, my God... *(Staring round, taking it in.)* This is remarkable...

LILY. Do you like it?

ROB. ...quite remarkable... This isn't – this isn't some sort of film set, is it?

LILY. Pardon?

ROB. *(Shaking his head, incredulously.)* Some sort of windup?

LILY. *(Proudly.)* No, it's all custom-built. My husband, Alfie, fitted it himself – most of it. He's clever with his hands.

ROB. What is he? A prop man? *(Examining more closely.)* It all seems perfectly authentic, too.

LILY. *(With a sudden gush of enthusiasm.)* Oh, yes, it's all up-to-the-minute, you know, with Alfie's family being in the business, of course. I mean, we had contacts through the family firm, Tindle's. They're very well connected are Tindle's. In the trade. We could get hold of practically anything through Alf's dad, Reg. In the old days, of course. No, I must say, it's paid off for us being Tindle's. When we were setting up house, seven years ago, we could get anything we wanted, practically. At least, we used to. Different now of course, these days. Still. What do they say? We must all tighten our belts, mustn't we?

ROB. *(A little taken aback by this onslaught.)* Quite so. Yes. We need to beat this thing, don't we?

LILY. Yes, the bastards! *(Warming to her subject.)* I mean, this stove for instance, seven years since we bought it, I can't count the number of meals I must've cooked on it, it's still as good as new. It's a joy to clean, sheer joy. How much do you think we paid for it? Go on, have a guess?

ROB. No idea.

LILY. Guess.

ROB. Well. Fifty quid?

LILY. Fifty? Did you say fifty? What, pounds? Fifty pounds?

ROB. Well, possibly a bit more, collectors' item. Seventy-five, perhaps?

LILY. *(Laughing.)* Where have you been living, Tiger? Come down off your ladder, Mr Fireman, into the real world. I'll tell you. Five pounds, ten shillings.

ROB. Good God!

LILY. And that came ready connected and all.

ROB. Amazing.

LILY. They did that for free. And that's all thanks to Tindle's, that is.

ROB. This Tindle's. I'm not sure I'm familiar with them…?

LILY. Tindle's. You must know Tindle's. Big shop on the corner. Right at the top end of Pike Street. Just before you turn into Willoughby. Big shop, you can't miss it. Tindle & Son. Ironmongers.

ROB. Oh, yes, of course. Where the MacDonald's is...

(He looks around him with increasing desperation. He is sinking fast.)

Look, Lily, this may sound a silly question but...

LILY. What, go on?

ROB. ... I mean, I feel a bit stupid even asking it, but...

LILY. No, go on, what?

ROB. Well, where's the door? What have you done with your door?

LILY. Pardon?

ROB. I just can't see a door anywhere, that's all. I mean, unless your husband has been particularly clever with his hands, I can't quite see where you've hidden it...

LILY. I don't quite follow. The door's behind you.

ROB. Yes. No, that's the garden door we just came through. I didn't mean that one. I meant the other door. You must have another door? Leading to the rest of the house? Where's that?

LILY. *(Pointing.)* It's over there, isn't it?

ROB. *(Straining to see it.)* Where?

LILY. *(Moving to stand in the doorway.)* Over here. Look, I'm standing in the doorway. You must be able to see it? Surely?

ROB. *(Who clearly can't.)* Yes. Yes. Would you mind doing me a favour – would you possibly mind walking through it – just to put my mind at ease, you know.

LILY. *(Smiling.)* You want me to walk through this doorway?

ROB. If you'd be so kind.

LILY. What, into the hall, you mean?

ROB. If you would.

LILY. You're not going to get up to mischief in here, are you?

ROB. *(Laughing nervously.)* No. Promise I won't try and steal your stove.

LILY. I think you're slightly mad, you know.

ROB. I think I must be. Six years of twice weekly episodes has finally taken its toll. My much learning hath made me mad...

LILY. It must have done. Here I go, then. Bye-bye.

*(**LILY** steps through the doorway.)*

*(For **ROB** she has abruptly vanished.)*

ROB. *(Clutching his heart and sitting.)* Oh, dear God! She's vanished! Completely vanished! What's happening to me? What the hell's happening to me?

*(He drags his head between his knees and takes a series of short panting breaths. **LILY** returns holding a leaflet.)*

LILY. *(Looking at him, concerned.)* You alright, Tiger, are you?

ROB. Yes, fine. Felt a little faint, that's all...

LILY. If you don't mind me saying so, for a fireman, you're a bit of a disappointment. I thought you were all as tough as nails, you lot.

ROB. Yes, well, you shouldn't believe everything you see on – that you haven't yet seen. What have you got there?

LILY. Just come through the letterbox. *(Studying her leaflet.)* Oh, this'll be useful. I'm pleased he remembered to drop one in. Very thoughtful of him.

ROB. Who's that?

LILY. Mr Rogers.

ROB. Who's Mr Rogers?

LILY. Mr Rogers. Our warden. You must know Mr Rogers, surely?

ROB. Oh, heavens, yes. That Mr Rogers.

LILY. Left this leaflet for me. He promised he would.

ROB. *(Reaching out his hand.)* May I?

LILY. *(Handing it to him.)* Here. I'm sure you know it all, already.

ROB. *(Reading, with increasing incredulity.)* "A concise, fully illustrated and Practical Guide for the householder and Air-Raid Warden. Officially recommended by the Air Raid Defence League. Price 7 ½d… *(He pauses.)* What date do you think it is, Lily? Today?

LILY. Oh, what'll it be today –? Let me see. August the fifth, isn't it?

ROB. Fifth of August, yes. It's the Fifth of August for me, too.

LILY. That's handy.

ROB. And what year are you – what year is it now, do you think?

LILY. *(Now very concerned.)* Oh, dear. You poor thing, you're suffering from shock, aren't you? It's shock, that's what it is. Now, don't worry, you're not to worry.

It happens to lots of people, it's nothing to be ashamed of. You mustn't let it get you down, darling. You must try and get over it. We're relying on people like you, you know. Heroes like you and my Alfie. Don't you start falling apart on us now. You're our frontline, you are. We need you. We need you to be strong for us.

(She sits beside him and pats his hand encouragingly.)

(Gently.) If it's any help, if it makes you feel any better, it's 1942, darling.

ROB. *(Softly.)* Oh, help! Help!

LILY. I'll put the kettle on, make us both a nice cup of tea. Alright? Like a nice cup of tea would you, Tiger? Yes. I'll make us a pot. Auntie Gladys can wait. She won't miss me. She never knows what time it is half the time, anyway.

*(As **LILY** busies herself making tea in the teapot, **ROB** continues to sit there and watch her.)*

(Filling the kettle.) Oh, this wretched tap! *(Struggling.)* It turns on alright, but I can never get it to turn off proper. I think it must be the washer.

ROB. *(Rising.)* Oh, yes. Forgot why I was here. Here. Let me...

LILY. Oh, thank you. Needs a strong man, that's all.

*(**ROB** turns off the tap relatively easily.)*

ROB. There you go.

LILY. Look at that. All it takes. Easy as pie. Times like this when I – ooh – I really wish I was a man, you know.

ROB. I think you're perfect the way you are.

LILY. Careful now! Behave yourself, Tiger. You'll have your wife after you, otherwise. *(She laughs.)* I take it you've got a wife, have you?

ROB. Yes.

LILY. With you next door, is she? Staying at Elsie's with you?

ROB. No, she's – she's not with me at present.

LILY. Not there to keep an eye on you, then?

ROB. Quite frankly, I don't think my wife would be bothered one way or the other.

LILY. What, your wife? I bet she would be.

ROB. Not really.

LILY. I bet she cares. I bet she does. Underneath, I bet she's really proud of you.

ROB. You'd never have known it…

LILY. I bet she is. Secretly. She just never says it. Women are like that. We try not to praise you men too much in case you get big headed. Like when Alfie'd finished putting in this kitchen, he said, "There you are, what you think, Lil?" And I said, "Not bad, it'll do." And you should have seen his face, it practically fell through the floor. He looked so disappointed, I had to kiss him. Kiss him better. Tell him I was only joking.

ROB. I don't think that's likely to happen in my case.

LILY. Just wait till her house is on fire and you come busting through the window to rescue her, that's all I can say.

ROB. She'd probably have started the fire in the first place…

(He breaks off, shaking his head.)

*(He realises he may have upset **LILY**.)*

Sorry. Sorry, Lily, I didn't mean to…

LILY. You're staying on your own then? At Mrs Doggett's, are you?

ROB. No, I'm currently with my sister.

LILY. Oh, your sister? That's nice.

ROB. I have the – spare room. You know.

LILY. What are you? A relative of Mrs Doggett's, are you?

ROB. Yes, I'm her – nephew. She's my aunt. I've just been – relocated locally. And I finished up, as luck would have it, with dear old aunt – Enid.

LILY. Elsie. I think her name's Elsie.

ROB. Elsie! Of course, Elsie. I've got so many aunts, you've no idea. Aunts coming out of my ears. *(Anxious to change the subject.)* So, you're a local family, I take it?

LILY. *(As she busies herself.)* Oh, yes. My dad was a postman and my mum were a schoolmistress before the war. Both of them departed now, sadly.

ROB. Oh. Was that the result of…?

LILY. Last October. Air raid. Tube station. Direct hit.

ROB. I'm so sorry.

LILY. At least they went together. That's what they'd have wanted. Most of Alfie's family are still with us, anyway. His parents, Reg and Maude, they're both very hearty. Running the shop between them, these days. Since the boys got called up.

ROB. This is the ironmongers?

LILY. Tindle's, yes. I worked there for a bit before I was married. On the till mostly. That's how I met Alfie. Then Reg bought us this place as a wedding present, and we did it up. And then along came Charlie and little Connie. And we were all happy as Larry. Until this blessed war came along and spoilt it all.

ROB. And Alfie's overseas, you say?

LILY. Somewhere. They can never tell you where though, can they? All I know is he's Fifth Royal Tanks. Tank commander. Sergeant. Somewhere or other. He's due some leave soon. Any day now. Can't wait! Be wonderful to see him again. He won't get to see the kids though. They won't be around, of course.

ROB. Oh, are they…?

LILY. Evacuees, yes. Alfie and I thought it best they didn't stop here. It was no place for young children, London. I mean Connie's only six and Charlie's only a year older. It wasn't right for them to be here, not at that age. Not with all the bombs. I couldn't go with them, of course, with the family here. They all need looking after, too, in their own way. I miss them both so much. I worry they're being looked after properly. That they've been kept together, you know. I like to think they're both on a farm somewhere together, feeding the animals, you know. But you hear stories, don't you? That the farmers sometimes split them up because they only want strong-looking boys who can work, and they send the girls off somewhere else. Which I think is a bit unfair, really. Cos girls can work too, can't they? Just as hard as boys.

> *(She has set out the tea things, warmed the pot, carefully spooned loose leaves into the teapot and poured in boiling water.)*

There we are. Leave it to brew. You take it strong, Tiger, do you?

ROB. Reasonably.

LILY. Alfie likes it strong. As for Reg, his dad, you can stand your spoon up in it.

> *(They sit and wait.)*

Do you have any children?

ROB. Just the one. A daughter, Ali. She's just started teaching at York University.

LILY. Ali? Short for Alison, is it?

ROB. Alisha.

LILY. Alisha? That's unusual.

ROB. It's Indian. Her mother was part Indian, you know.

LILY. Ah, foreign then, is she?

ROB. Well, when it comes down to it, we're all of us slightly foreign, aren't we?

LILY. I'm not foreign. English and proud of it, me.

ROB. *(Guardedly.)* Yes. I think somehow that's probably a conversation for another year… Think it's brewed enough, do you?

LILY. Oh, yes, don't want it stewed, do we? Waste of precious tea, otherwise. Now, would you like milk with it…?

ROB. Just a drop, thanks…

LILY. …because I don't have fresh, I'm afraid. I always give mine straight to Reg and Maude. Reg loves his cup of tea and besides, I can never keep milk fresh enough here, it curdles soon as look at it, so there's only powdered. Do you mind powdered?

ROB. There's no chance of a slice of lem – no, this'll be fine, I'll just drink it neat. Perfect.

LILY. Sure?

ROB. Lovely.

(He sips the tea.)

LILY. I hope you don't take sugar, because –

ROB. *(Hastily interrupting her.)* No, no, no! No sugar, thank you!

LILY. – I'm running low on that, as well. Auntie Gladys has a very sweet tooth.

ROB. I must say, you're extremely generous with your rations, giving them all away.

LILY. They're family, aren't they? You have to look after them…

ROB. You need to look after yourself, as well, Lily.

LILY. Oh, I can manage. Besides, I'm one of the lucky ones, aren't I? If the house burns down, I've got my very own fireman living next door, haven't I?

(She smiles at him.)

(He smiles back at her.)

Even if he can't find the door.

*(From outside, the wailing siren of an air raid warning sounds. **ROB** is startled.)*

Oh, no! Not again! Would you credit it? The minute you sit down for a cup of tea… *(Rising and moving to the garden door.)* Come on!

ROB. What's going on? What are we doing?

LILY. Quickly! Air raid! Leave your tea! I swear, they can hear the kettle boiling! Reg says those Germans, they've got listening machines everywhere… *(Impatiently.)* Come on, Tiger, you coming?

ROB. *(Slightly confused.)* Where are we going?

LILY. The shelter! Come on!

ROB. What? In that thing? We can't both hide in that thing, there's hardly suitable social distan –

(Somewhere nearby, a sudden explosion.)

Oh, my God!

LILY. *(Urgently.)* Tiger! Please! Come on!

(**ROB** *dithers uncertainly.*)

(**LILY** *goes off to the shelter.*)

(*Another explosion, closer this time, panics* **ROB** *into a decision.*)

ROB. Oh, Jesus! This can't be happening!

(*He makes a panicky run for the shelter.*)

(*As he goes.*) What's happening? This can't be happening to me!

(*A series of further explosions, some of them very close indeed as the lights fade to: –*)

(*A blackout.*)

End of Scene One

Scene Two

(That evening.)

*(In the kitchen of number 15, **ALEX** sitting at her laptop.)*

*(**ROB** has evidently just delivered an account of his morning's adventure.)*

ALEX. *(Taken aback.)* My God!

ROB. In a nutshell.

ALEX. Good Lord.

ROB. Believe it or not.

ALEX. I'm not quite sure that I do, Rob. Not really.

ROB. Well, you asked me.

ALEX. All I said was, have you had a busy day? And then you come out with all that. I never expected all that.

ROB. I can't say I expected it either. When I first walked out of that door this morning to talk to her, I never expected –

ALEX. No, please, Rob, no! Please, don't start all over again, please! Once round is quite enough! I've had the most stressful day as it is. This new Chancellor's completely hopeless. I don't think she can even add up properly…

ROB. One of the pre-requisites of the job, isn't it? For Chancellor of the Exchequer?

ALEX. You'd think so, wouldn't you?

ROB. Like having a Transport Minister with travel sickness, isn't it? A colour-blind Minister for the Arts – oh no, hang on, we've had plenty of them, already.

ALEX. Well, I'll say this, Rob, I've always appreciated having a brother like you. After a gruelling day coping with grim reality, it's good to get back to you. To be taken out of myself for a moment. When we were kids and I'd fallen off my bike or something, you were always there with some wonderful story, some magical adventure with pirates and princesses and dragons – or whatever – you were always there, weren't you, to carry me off to another world. It must be wonderful to have that sort of mind. That imagination. I did so envy you sometimes. By comparison, my world is so boring and practical and dull, so bloody down-to-earth. In my world, everything needs to have a purpose. I took after daddy. God, did I take after him? He was such a deeply boring man, wasn't he? He'd send roomfuls of people to sleep with his endless lists of statistics and little-known facts. And that's me too, I'm afraid. Whilst you and Mummy were in the other room enjoying amazing adventures you'd made up in your heads... Oh, you're so lucky, you know. Whilst the rest of us shuffle along, heads down, eyes fixed firmly on a pavement of practicality, you just sail away, don't you, dreaming up your life as you go along...

ROB. Alex, if I could just interrupt, darling, for one second –

ALEX. Sorry?

ROB. What I told you just then was not a story. It was the truth. It was God's honest truth. Every single word of it. I promise.

(She stares at him for a moment.)

(She smiles and shakes her head.)

ALEX. No, I'm not falling for that again. Sorry. You can't catch me any more. Ever since that time you convinced me there were crocodiles in the bath and I couldn't wash for weeks… Well, let me tell you something, Robert Hathaway. I phoned Ian Taylor at lunchtime…

ROB. Ian Taylor?

ALEX. The keyholder of number 17. The Jessops' nephew. I asked him if he wouldn't mind checking the property and if necessary, report back to the Jessops, which the dear man conscientiously did, risking a heavy fine I may add, checking upstairs and downstairs including the kitchen and the garden and he rang me back an hour later to say he could see no sign of a disturbance and everything seemed present and correct. So, you can't fool me, brother dear.

ROB. Which door did he use to get in?

ALEX. The front door, of course. He had the key.

ROB. He should have gone in through the back door, through the kitchen.

ALEX. Ah, but if he had, according to you, in order to check the rest of the house, he'd have had to walk clean through the kitchen wall, wouldn't he? You see there are holes in your story, dear brother. We are not quite so gullible, we life plodders, as we used to be.

ROB. Yes, I thought you might say that so, on behalf of life's dreamers, I got practical, too. I'll have you know I spent most of the afternoon upstairs in my bedroom on my laptop. Checking her story.

ALEX. Really? OK, convince me.

ROB. Most of what she said checks out. True, before the war, there used to be a big ironmongers on the corner of Pike Street and Willoughby. Tindle & Son. So that bit's true…

ALEX. Well, surprise! Maybe she's got a computer, as well…

ROB. *(Ignoring her.)* …the proprietor was indeed Reginald Arthur Tindle, born 1885, died 1962. His wife and partner Maude Irene, born 1887, died 1978. His only son, Alfred William Jonas Tindle, born 1915 –

ALEX. *(Impatiently.)* Darling, this is brilliantly impressive. But she could just as easily have looked all this up online for herself –

ROB. No, no, wait! ...his only son, Alfred William Jonas, born 1915, Fifth Royal Tank Regiment, killed in action El Alamein, 1942 –

ALEX. – looked all this up first and then made up the story –

ROB. – listen! El Alamein was in July 1942. It was all over and done with by July 27th. We're now well into August, aren't we? Which means he must already be dead.

ALEX. Well, that's blown a hole in her story then, hasn't it? She should have checked that, shouldn't she?

ROB. I don't think she knows. I don't think she's yet been told. These things took time in those days. Before families were officially notified. For her it's the fifth of August, same date as us. So in her time, he's only been dead a few days. No one's broken the news to her yet. She's still expecting him home on leave, any day now. God, who's going to tell her? I can't possibly tell her.

ALEX. At the risk of getting myself involved in this ridiculous... If you don't mind my asking, who does she think you are precisely? A time traveller from the future?

ROB. No – she – she thinks I'm – she thinks I'm a fireman from the *NFS*.

ALEX. The *NFS*? What, off the telly?

ROB. No, she thinks I'm the real thing, the genuine item...

ALEX. My God, darling, she's a stalker. She's one of those demented fans. The ones you used to get so worried about. The ones who sent you anonymous letters you frame and hang up in downstairs loos. Do be careful, won't you?

ROB. No, this is different...

ALEX. You've had stalkers before, haven't you? Remember that one, years ago, the one you always suspected was trying to break up your first marriage?

ROB. *(Scowling.)* Oh, that one.

ALEX. The one you always claimed deliberately blew the whistle on every single affair you had...

ROB. Bloody right she was, broke up our marriage, that one. Either that or Anya employed a private detective, I wouldn't have put it past her...

ALEX. Darling, the reason Anya divorced you was that A, she was no fool and B, she could read you like a book.

ROB. Rubbish.

ALEX. Rob, everybody can. Which is probably one of the reasons you're such a good actor, darling. Everyone can tell immediately exactly what you're thinking. Which is terribly useful when you're performing, but not so good in real life when you're playing around behind your wife's back. Look, I must go back up. I promised I'd Skype Janice. Provided she's managed to get her mother into bed safely. As soon as I'm through, I'll pop back and make us dinner. Alright? I'm afraid it's another M&S instant again but you quite enjoy those, don't you? Did you get yourself any lunch, by the way...?

ROB. No, I –

ALEX. Oh, no, of course, you were both in your Anderson shelter, hiding from the air raid, I remember now. *(Kindly.)* Listen, darling, as a tiny precaution do lock all doors and windows down here, if you're at all nervous. I'd suggest you call the police but if you told them the story you've just told me, they'll probably lock you up. Don't worry. Soon be dinner time.

(**ALEX** *goes out.*)

(**ROB** *stands concerned.*)

ROB. *(To himself.)* She thinks I'm potty. She thinks I'm completely off my bloody rocker. Didn't believe a single word I – did I really dream all that up? Dear Lord! Maybe I've finally lost it? After all, I've turned sixty, haven't I? Is this the first sign? Am I finally descending the ultimate downward slope?

(*At number 17,* **LILY** *has stepped out of her kitchen door into the garden and stands taking in the evening air. She wears a whistle hanging from a lanyard round her neck.*)

Oh, thank God! She's back. She's still real. At least for now.

(*He tentatively comes out into his own garden.*)

Hello, there!

LILY. *(Coolly.)* Hello. How's Elsie, then?

ROB. Sorry, who?

LILY. Elsie? Your auntie?

ROB. Oh, she's fine. Auntie's fine.

LILY. *(Staring at him.)* Yes, I'm sure she is. She was right as rain half an hour ago…

ROB. *(Startled.)* Sorry?

LILY. …when I looked in on my way home from my auntie. Auntie Gladys. Who's real, by the way.

ROB. Oh.

LILY. Unlike your Auntie Elsie. Who's never heard of you. Who hasn't even got a nephew...

ROB. Yes. Lily, I need to explain that...

LILY. I think you do, yes. You owe me an explanation. I trusted you.

ROB. I'm sorry.

LILY. I told my father-in-law about you. About this fireman who'd moved in next door. He said you sounded fishy. He's no fool is Reg. Saw through you straight away without even looking at you. He said, if I saw you again, I'd do right to turn you in. He said you'd most likely parachuted onto Hampstead Heath. Some hero you are, Tiger George Jennings or whatever you call yourself...

ROB. No, I confess that's not my real name...

LILY. What is it, then? Otto von Stickleback?

ROB. No, it's Robert. Robert Hathaway.

LILY. Robert? Sure? How do I know that's even real?

ROB. It is, believe me. Robert. Rob to my friends.

LILY. I don't imagine you've got many of them, have you? *(Suddenly tearful.)* I'm so disappointed, you've no idea. I trusted you. I really believed you were a hero, like my Alfie...

ROB. I'm sorry. I'm not a hero. I'm no sort of hero...

LILY. No, you're a liar and a cheat, aren't you? How can I believe a single word you say to me ever again? You're not even a proper fireman, are you?

ROB. I'm afraid not, no. If you must know I'm an actor.

LILY. Didn't think you were a proper fireman. Down in that Anderson shelter, during that air raid, you were practically pissing yourself, weren't you?

ROB. Well, it did take me rather by surprise...

LILY. *(Dryly.)* Yes, well that's rather the point of them, air raids, isn't it? They don't usually send you a postcard first.

ROB. Listen, Lily, I'm going to be perfectly straight with you –

LILY. Oh, here it comes! When a bloke says that to you, it usually means he's about to tell you a load of porkies…

ROB. No, hear me out, Lily, please…

LILY. Go on, then. I'll help get you started, shall I? You're originally from Mars, aren't you…?

ROB. No, come on, be reasonable, you have to listen to me, Lily. I'm trying to explain it to you, the best way I can – Look, it's impossible talking to you over this stupid hedge. Tell you what, let me come round there and –

LILY. *(Fiercely.)* Oh, no, you don't! I'll tell you what, you keep your side, I'll stay mine, alright? You're not setting foot in this garden, never again.

ROB. *(Stepping back.)* Alright! All right! I'll stay here.

LILY. Do that!

ROB. *(With difficulty.)* Listen, there is something – happening here – how can I best put it? –

LILY. Oh, yes…?

ROB. – which is – virtually impossible –

LILY. …hark at him, just hark at him…

ROB. – in logical terms –

LILY. …making it up as he goes along, isn't he…?

ROB. *(Soldiering on.)* …to explain in words of one –

LILY. …and another thing…

ROB. *(Irritably.)* Please, allow me to finish –?

LILY. …you keep your hands where I can see them…

ROB. Why? What are you talking about now?

LILY. In case you've got a gun –

ROB. *(Angrily.)* Listen, if I had a gun, I'd have shot you through this hedge ten minutes ago! Now please, let me finish!

(A brief pause.)

Where was I? Lost my thread...

LILY. You were saying it's impossible to explain...

ROB. In rational terms, certainly. I think, Lily – what we're experiencing here – and I do know a little bit about these things, I did a couple of episodes of *Doctor Who* in the early days –

LILY. *(Baffled.)* What?

ROB. – what we are experiencing here is what is termed some form of a space time anomaly – in simple terms, what we are experiencing, both of us, is – basically – a tear in the basic temporal fabric... If you follow me.

LILY. No, I don't follow you at all. I haven't a clue what you're talking about. A tear in the fabric? That would explain why you appear to be talking out of the seat of your trousers, would it?

ROB. *(Hopelessly out of his depth.)* No, no, no. A tear in the fabric of the – space-time – continuum.

LILY. *(Half to herself.)* Barking. He's completely barking.

ROB. Where you are standing now, in your garden, it is August 1942. You are currently in the midst of what later became referred to as World War Two ...

LILY. Thanks for reminding me, I wondered where I was...

ROB. Whereas I – on this side of this hedge – I am for you, years in the future. Years and years. I don't know,

I can't do the maths – seventy-five? – seventy-eight years – in the future. Your future.

*(**LILY** stares at him.)*

Look, let me put it another way…

LILY. Please do.

ROB. This morning, when I stepped through this hedge, I travelled back in time – however many years that was – into my past. But my past, you see, is your present. Whereas if you stepped through this hedge into my garden…

LILY. Which I certainly don't intend to do…

ROB. …you would be stepping into my present, a present which is, in effect, your future. It's perfectly simple… *(A pause.)* Believe me, it's the only possible explanation.

*(**LILY** continues to stare at him.)*

LILY. Another possible explanation is that you're completely bonkers. That's another possibility.

ROB. If I could only… If I could only persuade you to step this side – just for a minute – I could convince you. You could see for yourself that I'm not lying. I'm not making all this up… I could show you my kitchen…

LILY. Your kitchen?

ROB. I'm sure that would convince you…

LILY. You want to show me your kitchen, now, do you?

ROB. Just a quick look. That's all it would take.

LILY. Makes a change from etchings. *(Cautiously.)* Alright. But if I do step over into my present your future…

ROB. No, <u>my</u> present <u>your</u> future…

LILY. That's what I said. I warn you, I'm bringing my whistle.

ROB. Your what?

LILY. *(Indicating.)* This whistle. The one our warden, Mr Rogers, gave me.

ROB. Ah, I see.

LILY. He said in these desperate times, a woman on her own needs a whistle.

ROB. Sound advice.

LILY. Right. I'm coming through. I warn you though try anything funny and I'm blowing it…

> (**LILY** *steps cautiously through the hedge and into the other garden.*)

ROB. *(Watching her.)* Alright?

LILY. Well. It doesn't feel much different.

ROB. It won't do. It didn't for me. *(Indicating the kitchen door.)* This way then.

LILY. After you. I've still got my whistle, remember.

> (**ROB** *leads the way to his kitchen door which he opens and invites her inside. Never taking her eyes off him, she enters the room, forcing him to retreat round the other side of the kitchen table. Finally, she takes a long look round the evidently unfamiliar room.*)

(Suspiciously.) What's all this, then? What is it?

> (*During the next,* **ROB** *slowly walks round the kitchen indicating, opening, and displaying each item in turn like a white goods salesman.*)

> (**LILY***'s expression gradually grows more incredulous.*)

ROB. Welcome to my kitchen. This – is my fridge – my refrigerator. Which keeps things cold. This is my freezer – which keeps things even colder. This – is my dishwasher – which does the washing up. This is my washing machine which washes all my clothes and so on. This is my spin dryer – which dries my clothes. This is my microwave – which cooks things rather quickly if you're in a hurry. This is my stove with its induction hob and its conventional gas oven – fan assisted, of course – and – that's about it. *(He pats the table.)* Kitchen table.

> *(**LILY** stands in the doorway, rendered speechless. She stares from one item to the other as she retraces, in her mind, her guided tour.)*

LILY. *(At last.)* So what do you find to do all day, then?

ROB. Well... I'm busy pressing buttons, you know. That and phoning men to come and fix things when they go wrong. Which they frequently do. Thanks to the march of progress, two steps forward, four steps sideways, one step backwards. Seen enough, have you?

LILY. It's terrifying. All this. Terrifying. I think I prefer mine. At least I know what's going on cos it's me doing it. With this lot, I'd be frightened to turn my back.

ROB. Are you convinced? Have I convinced you?

LILY. Yes, I'm convinced. Thanks very much. If you'll excuse me, I must get back to my own kitchen and put the kettle on. I need a cuppa after that to steady my nerves...

ROB. *(A sudden idea.)* Hang on! Wait there! Just one moment! Won't be a second! Be right back!

> *(He takes a step backwards through the doorway behind him which gives **LILY** the impression that, like she did earlier, **ROB** has disappeared through the wall.)*

LILY. Oh, dear God! He walked through the wall! He walked straight through the bloody wall. I'm going as barmy as he is. *(Staring round the room.)* If this is the future, you can keep it, mate.

> *(**ROB** apparently materialises again with a bottle of cognac and two large brandy glasses.)*

ROB. *(As he appears, triumphantly.)* Eureka!

> *(**LILY** reacts at his sudden reappearance.)*

LILY. *(Clutching her heart.)* Oh, don't do that to me!

ROB. What's the matter? Ah! Of course. Did I suddenly appear to disappear, just now?

> *(**LILY** nods.)*

And then I suddenly appeared to reappear?

> *(**LILY** nods.)*

Interesting. That's extremely interesting.

LILY. One way of putting it.

ROB. This morning, you know, exactly the same thing happened next door when you went into your hall...

LILY. What, I appeared to disappear, as well?

ROB. Quite. And then just as suddenly you appear to reappear.

LILY. No wonder you came over queer. Don't blame you. My heart's racing like a greyhound. *(She pats her chest.)*

ROB. Not to worry. *(Holding up the bottle.)* I brought something to calm our nerves.

LILY. What's that?

ROB. A little present from the future. Something I don't think you'll be enjoying that much back in your present. Cognac.

LILY. Come again?

ROB. Brandy. French. You fancy a drop of brandy?

LILY. I certainly would...

ROB. Grand.

LILY. ... I don't normally but...

ROB. Your place or mine?

LILY. *(Promptly.)* My place. Can't drink in here, can we? It'd be like drinking in an operating theatre...

ROB. Your place it is. If you don't object to me coming with you.

LILY. I still got my whistle, remember.

ROB. I don't want to worry you but if you blew it here and now, the only people likely to hear it would be Mr Rogers' grandchildren.

LILY. Oh, blimey! Better get back then, hadn't I?

ROB. You better had.

> (**LILY** *leads the way back through* **ROB***'s garden. The moment she steps outside the back door, all his security lights trip in, illuminating just his side of the hedge.* **LILY** *immediately flattens herself to the ground.)*

LILY. *(Yelling.)* Searchlights! Take cover!

ROB. What are you doing?

LILY. Searchlights!

ROB. Searchlights?

LILY. Get your head down!

ROB. They're my security lights, that's all. You're perfectly safe.

LILY. *(Raising her head a fraction.)* Security lights?

ROB. They usually activate, round about this time. Don't worry, they're on a timer. They'll go off in a second or two.

LILY. They better had, or we'll be done for major blackout violation.

> *(The lights cut out again abruptly.)*

ROB. There you are, you see. They won't come on again, providing we don't either of us make any big sudden movements. Move ahead gently and slowly... That's it... Gently... Gently...

> *(**LILY** slowly gropes her way towards the gap in the hedge.)*

LILY. *(As she does so.)* Can't see a thing, now...

> *(She eases her way through the gap in the fence. **ROB** follows her. They both move cautiously to avoid triggering the sensor.)*

(Catching herself on the hedge.) Ow!

ROB. *(Doing likewise.)* Ouch! It is dark, isn't it?

LILY. On our side of this hedge, I'll have you know, we happen to be law-abiding citizens.

> *(They pick their way across her garden and enter her kitchen.)*

Wait, while I do the curtains.

> *(In the darkness, she adjusts the window blackout while **ROB** waits.)*

Right. Shut the door so I can do the light.

> *(He does so. **LILY** switches on the bright overhead light. Her kitchen appears sadly dingy after the gleaming high-tech showcase next door.)*

(A pause while she looks round.)

(Resignedly.) Well, at least it's home.

ROB. It's – it's very cosy.

LILY. Cosy. Yes.

(Slight pause.)

I couldn't live in that one next door, I'm sorry. Not for five minutes, I couldn't. I mean, it's very nice but it's not somewhere you could sit down and enjoy a cuppa, is it?

ROB. Now then – *(Proffering the bottle.)* – a glass of this, then?

LILY. *(Eyeing the brandy balloon suspiciously.)* I hope you're not expecting me to drink that whole glassful, are you? A very small one, just a drop at the bottom.

ROB. That's all you're getting.

(He pours them both a regulation drop.)

LILY. That'll do! Ta. Pour yourself a proper glass if you like. Don't let me stop you.

ROB. No, this is fine. Good health.

LILY. Cheers. *(She sips it.)*

ROB. Nice?

LILY. Very nice. You know this always reminds me of when I was ill as a kid. Gran always used to mix a drop of brandy with hot milk. Teaspoon of honey. Gran's remedy. *(Draining her glass.)* Yes, this is very nice, I could get used to this…

ROB. Drop more?

LILY. Just a drop. I mean don't get me wrong, I didn't mean to be rude about your kitchen. Each one to his own, eh?

So long as your wife's happy working in it, that's what matters, isn't it? So long as she's happy, that's the point.

ROB. *(Puzzled.)* My wife?

LILY. After all, her kitchen's a reflection of a woman's personality, isn't it? Now this room, this says me. I chose this. This is my space. While that room, yours next door, that says her, doesn't it? Your wife?

ROB. I don't think it does you know. Far more likely, it says me.

LILY. You?

ROB. I chose all that. Nothing to do with her, at all. I don't think June ever spent more than twenty minutes in it, all the time she lived there.

LILY. She didn't?

ROB. I did most of the cooking. When we weren't eating out. June was never a woman you'd describe as a domestic goddess. Her interests lay elsewhere. Whereas, on the other hand, there's nothing I enjoy more, when I'm not working that is, than whipping up a cheese soufflé. But June was – my second wife was – let's just say, these days – *(Indicating next door.)* – in these days, women's interests have rather branched out.

LILY. So have men's, from the sound of it. I can't see my Alfie ever whipping up a cheese soufflé. Did your second wife die then?

ROB. Sorry? What makes you think that?

LILY. It's just you keep talking about her as if she'd passed on?

ROB. In a way she has, yes.

LILY. Ah! Gone to a better place, has she?

ROB. She probably believes she has, yes. Time will tell, won't it? Knowing the bloke she moved in with, I somehow doubt it. She and I, we've been separated fourteen years. Only recently finalised the divorce. Recently? God, two years ago now.

LILY. That's a terrible thing for a woman to do, carry on behind her husband's back. I could never do that to Alfie. I told him the day he went off to war. I'd always be here for him. However long this went on for. Me and the kids, we'd be here when he came back. *(Shaking her head.)* I could never do that to my husband. It's a sin in a way, isn't it? Would you mind if I had another drop? Do you mind?

ROB. No, of course, I'm sorry. *(He hastily pours her some more.)*

LILY. You're a bit stingy with it, aren't you? You can pour us a bit more than that. No, I think it was terrible of her, walking out on you, like that.

ROB. *(Slightly guiltily.)* Well, to be fair, it was a bit – six of one. She wasn't entirely to blame – I – I admit I played my part, as well.

LILY. Well, you would do, you were probably lonely weren't you, her being off all the time? Don't blame you. Serve her right.

ROB. Believe me, Lily, mine's not a good business to be in, sometimes. It puts a great strain on your – on a marriage.

LILY. June was your second wife, you say?

ROB. That's right.

LILY. Mind my asking, but was she a lot younger than you?

ROB. *(A little startled by this question.)* Yes. Fifteen years younger, as a matter of fact. Why do you ask?

LILY. Sounds as if she was, that's all. What about the first wife, what happened to her?

ROB. What, Anya?

LILY. Did she leave you, as well?

ROB. Yes, eventually. But that was entirely my own fault, I admit it. We married far too young, we were both kids, still at drama school. Neither of us could handle it. There she was, stuck at home with the baby, poor love, out of work, waiting for the phone to ring.

(He rises agitatedly and starts to pace the tiny kitchen. **LILY** *watches him, concerned.)*

And there was me, fifteen solid weeks on the road schlepping round the country with some run-of-the-mill sex comedy. Night after night, eight bloody shows a week. Cramped digs, so damned cold, we all took to sleeping in the same bloody bed most nights, just to keep warm. I tell you it would have taken the willpower of a castrated Jesuit priest, not to have... I'm afraid I blew it, Lily. I buggered the whole marriage. And that was it. End of marriage. Kaput! Fini!

(He sits, a broken man.)

*(***LILY*** pushes the bottle towards him.)*

(Pouring himself another.) Thank you. *(More muted.)* Same thing with my bloody career, you know, Lily. I blew that as well. Torpedoed it straight to the bottom of the pond. All I did was grab the bastard by the throat. I never meant to – My God, we never heard the end of it, did we? Industrial tribunals, BBC health and safety, the full might of Equity... Six years I gave them. Six of my prime years, Lily, I sacrificed for that lot. Ungrateful pen-pushers. I made three front covers you know, Lily. Three front covers of the Radio Times. Three consecutive years. That's practically the TV equivalent of a bloody knighthood. Tiger, our national hero. That's what it said on one of them. Our National Hero. Well. Soon forgotten, eh?

*(***LILY*** has been somewhat depressed by this.)*

(She helps herself to another glass.)

(He becomes aware of her silently sitting there.)

Sorry. Didn't mean to go on. Sorry to bore you, Lily. Come on, Robert, pull yourself together, man! This woman's in the middle of a war, isn't she? What the hell have I got to complain about? You've enough troubles of your own, darling, haven't you? Without me droning on…

LILY. *(Emerging from her own reverie.)* No, I was just wondering, how I'd feel if I found out Alfie was having a love affair. I'd be hurt, of course. It would be very painful. Don't get me wrong. It would hurt me terribly. But I think I could forgive him, you know. Because he's a man and I appreciate what he's going through. I don't just mean the war, that he's fighting a war and risking his life for us – but, in the end he's a man, isn't he? And men have these – needs – these urges.

ROB. I'm afraid they do, yes.

LILY. Like you had.

ROB. But don't women have similar needs and urges?

LILY. Well, yes, we certainly do, yes. But we control them, don't we?

ROB. Why? Why you and not us?

LILY. Because we have to, don't we? Oh, I know some girls, girls round here even, friends of mine, they're busy putting it about all over the place – but they're no better than they should be, are they? Should be ashamed of themselves. I'd never do that, not to Alfie. Mind you, I've been tempted, you know. Once or twice I've been tempted. The other day, this young feller come to the door, he was that attractive. He was so young and – couldn't have been more than Alfie's age – can't imagine why he wasn't called up. Must have had something wrong with him, I suppose. He had this beautiful mouth, you know – lovely shaped lips – I wished I'd had lips like his – I just wanted to grab hold of him and pull him towards me and – oh! *(She shivers.)* But I never did! I held myself back. I don't know what he'd have done if I'd – After all, he'd only come round to check my gas mask, hadn't he? ... Strong, isn't it, this stuff? *(Fanning her face, embarrassed.)* Look at me, I'm blushing now. I don't know why I told you that. I don't know what you must think of me...

ROB. I don't think we're that different, you know.

(He refills both their glasses.)

LILY. If you want my opinion, all you needed in your life was a good woman to look out for you properly...

ROB. Oh, there've been plenty of women...

LILY. *(Smiling.)* But none of them that good, from the sound of it, were they?

*(**ROB** smiles.)*

You still get tempted occasionally, do you?

ROB. *(Staring at her.)* Not if I can help it.

LILY. *(Staring at him.)* No?

ROB. Except for the times when I simply can't help it.

(He smiles and continues to stare at her.)

(She smiles back and shakes her head.)

(She holds up her hand and points significantly at her ring finger.)

LILY. Behave! Behave yourself, now!

ROB. *(Holding up a hand, apologetically.)* Sorry.

LILY. I told you, Alfie's due some leave any time. I had this postcard from him a week ago. He could walk in any minute. Then what would you do?

ROB. Probably beat a hasty retreat. As I said, I'm not much of a hero…

LILY. I could tell him you were whipping me up a cheese soufflé. Whatever that might be.

ROB. I think I'd find that a bit challenging on that stove…

LILY. Now, don't you be rude about Mervyn. I won't have a word said against my Mervyn…

ROB. Mervyn?

LILY. My stove.

ROB. You call your stove Mervyn?

LILY. I talk to him some mornings. "Mervyn, are you going to behave today? Or you going to burn things like you usually do? Boil everything over without warning me?"

ROB. Why on earth Mervyn?

LILY. Don't know. Teacher at school, I think. Domestic science. I give most things names. Always have done. That kettle there, that's Kevin. Kevin the kettle. And that cupboard over there, that's Clarissa. Alfie says I'm slightly mad. I think I probably am, you know.

ROB. *(Gently.)* I don't think you're mad. You're not mad.

LILY. Lonely, possibly.

ROB. I think you're lovely. Just lovely.

(They look at each other.)

(A silence between them.)

LILY. *(Softly, shaking her head.)* We mustn't. We really mustn't, you know.

(They continue to look at each other.)

ROB. No, we shouldn't. We shouldn't at all.

LILY. It wouldn't be right…

ROB. Completely wrong.

LILY. He could walk in here, any minute…

ROB. I don't think he will you know. It's very unlikely.

LILY. How do you – Oh my God, of course, you're from the future, aren't you? I should have thought. You must know everything, mustn't you? Everything that will happen, what's going to happen? You must know everything.

ROB. Well, not quite everything…

LILY. How long's this war going on for, then? Do you know that?

ROB. Well…

LILY. How long? Tell me.

ROB. A year or two yet…

LILY. *(Appalled.)* A <u>year</u> or two?

ROB. Soon be over.

LILY. A year or <u>two</u>? God, that's terrible! I can't put up with another two years of this. What's going to happen to us? What about my kids? Connie and Charlie? What's going to happen to them? Will they be alright?

ROB. *(Somewhat alarmed.)* Look, I really don't – I really can't possibly –

LILY. What about Alfie? Will he come home safe and sound?

ROB. *(Panicking.)* This isn't a good area to get into, you know. If I start warning you about things, telling you about things to look out for in the future – nothing good ever comes of it. We could alter the whole timeline.

LILY. Timeline? What are you talking about, what's a timeline?

ROB. Listen, years ago I was in an episode of *Star Trek* – nothing major, just a guest Romulan – two or three lines – but the point was he went on to warn someone about the future and so he changed it and of course it had this devastating knock-on effect and virtually destroyed the whole civilisation… The point is these are not things we should ever meddle in. We really shouldn't.

LILY. But can't you tell me about Alfie? What's going to happen?

ROB. No, I can't possibly go into… Not even if I knew. Which I don't. Quite truthfully, I don't. I can tell you general things like how long the war's going to last – broad details – I can warn you about Dunkirk – Oh, no – 1942 – that's been and gone, hasn't it – and you're over the Blitz, too, aren't you? Just about – the worst of it anyway – yes, you're over the hill, Lily, you're gradually winning – trust old Winston to see you through – one or two nasty things to come, though – V1's, doodlebugs, V2's and so on…

LILY. *(Horrified.)* Doodlebug's? Did you say, <u>Doodlebug</u>? What the hell are they?

ROB. *(Slightly deliriously.)* No, no, no! Look on the bright side. At least you've got the GIs to look forward to. They'll be here soon! Cheer up! Chewing gum, cigarettes, nylon stockings, Hershey bars and Glenn Miller…

LILY. I've no idea what you're talking about, I'm sorry. Truthfully. You don't know any of the details, then?

ROB. No. How could I – possibly?

LILY. Honest truth? You don't know nothing at all?

ROB. No.

LILY. *(Studying him.)* I don't believe you. You're not a very – I was going to say you're not a very good actor, but I think that might be a bit rude of me. But you're not.

ROB. *(Mildly offended.)* Yes, that's a matter of opinion, of course. I've had some pretty favourable reviews in my time, but never mind...

LILY. Sorry.

(A silence.)

*(**LILY** pours them both another drink.)*

What made you say, it's unlikely.

ROB. How do you mean?

LILY. When I told you, my husband could walk in at any minute, you said, it's very unlikely. What made you say that?

ROB. I've no idea – I – I was – hypothesising.

LILY. You were what?

ROB. I was supposing. I was simply putting forward the supposition. Based on what I knew –

LILY. What you knew? Then you do know something?

ROB. Based on what I knew of the trains. Of that period. This period. They were notoriously unreliable at this – time in history. So I read. Thanks to the bombing. Even more unreliable than they are today. My time. *(He laughs.)* Which is saying something. *(He laughs again.)*

LILY. You're still lying, aren't you? You're still not telling me the truth. Why can't you tell me the truth? What happened to Alfie? What's happened to him? Please. Tell me. Please.

(A slight pause.)

ROB. *(Blurting it out.)* He's dead, Lily. He's been killed in action. I'm so sorry.

LILY. *(Faintly, barely taking it in.)* What?

ROB. 1942. El Alemain. 5th Royal Tank regiment. Desert Rats. 22nd Armoured Brigade, 7th Armoured Division. Sergeant. Tank Commander. Posthumous George Cross medal for gallantry. I'm sorry. I didn't know how the hell to tell you. Sorry.

> (**LILY** *walks a little way away, breathing deeply, starting to hyperventilate, as the shock takes hold. Her breath begins to come out as barely audible suppressed whimpers.*)

(Watching her, concerned.) Lily? Lily? Lily...?

> (**LILY** *collapses as her knees give way suddenly and she clutches the edge of the table.*)

(Crying out in alarm.) LILY!!!

> *(He springs forward and half catches her before she can hit the floor. Her breathing sounds get louder.)*

> (**ROB**, *supporting her, lifts her onto the kitchen table. He pulls her close to him. She responds by clinging tightly, moaning into his chest. As they do this,* **ROB** *strokes her hair and murmurs reassuringly to her.*)

(Cooing softly in her ear.) It's all right, Lily, I've got you, lean on me, hold on to me, my darling, I've got you. Breathe slowly. Alright, it's alright! Slowly! That's it! Hold on to me, hold on to me, Lily darling, that's it!

> *(It is on this tableau, that* **ALF** *enters. In battledress, twenty-five years old, sunburnt, and extremely fit. He takes in the scene.* **ROB**, *seeing him, reacts in alarm as* **ALF**, *for him,*

has apparently emerged through the kitchen wall. **ROB** *pushes* **LILY** *from him and retreats into a far corner.)*

(As he does so.) Oh, dear God!

*(***LILY*** spins round and also catches sight of the newcomer.)*

LILY. *(With a stifled scream.)* Alfie!

(She faints away again and really does hit the floor this time. She lies unconscious in a crumpled heap.)

ALF. *(With quiet menace.)* Evening, mate. What the bloody hell are you playing at with my wife, then?

ROB. *(With a weak smile.)* Ah. Hello there.

*(As **ALF** starts to advance and **ROB** flattens himself further into the corner, the lights fade to a: –)*

(Blackout.)

End of Act One

ACT TWO

Scene One

(The same. The following afternoon.)

(Though the time is the same in both locations, the weather is markedly different. In the garden of number 17, the sky is overcast and it is raining. The garden there is deserted and desolate.)

(Whereas in the garden of number 15, things are brighter. A folding table with four chairs has been set up and evidence of an earlier barbecued meal having recently been consumed. Nearby is a cold box half filled with cans of beer. There is no sign of the actual barbecue itself as this is out of sight at the far end of this garden. From that direction can be heard the shouts of the two men as they indulge in some sporting activity. The August sun here shines down with not a cloud in the sky.)

*(A cry of despair from **ROB** and, in a moment, a football rolls into view, pursued by **ALF**, now out of uniform and evidently enjoying himself.)*

ALF. *(As he enters, calling.)* Three nil. To West Ham.

(*He gathers up the ball and runs off with it again.*)

(*Meanwhile, in the kitchen of number 17,* **LILY** *and* **ALEX** *have been saddled with the washing up, the former washing, the latter drying.*)

(*Whereas* **LILY** *is setting about her task with purposeful concentration, her companion appears less enamoured with the job.*)

(*She desultorily dries a plate as she stares out at the rain.*)

(*They are both dressed casually wearing trousers,* **LILY** *in slacks,* **ALEX** *in jeans.*)

ALEX. (*Sourly.*) This is all quaintly traditional, isn't it? Whilst the men happily romp in the sunshine, we're stuck in the kitchen, staring at the rain and doing the chores...

LILY. Well, they enjoy a game, don't they? Men? They're always playing at something or other, aren't they? When I worked at Tindle's, the lads there, they were always playing round the back in the lunch break. Cricket or football.

(*A joyous shout from* **ALF** *in the next door garden.*)

So long as they're enjoying themselves, that's the main thing. Men need to let off steam, now and then, don't they?

ALEX. (*Unenthusiastically.*) Yes?

LILY. Have you got a husband, have you?

ALEX. (*Startled.*) No.

LILY. Boyfriend?

ALEX. No.

LILY. *(Sympathetically.)* Ah. Never mind. Never too late, is it, they say? You'll be hearing wedding bells soon, I'm sure.

ALEX. I do hope not. I already have a wife.

LILY. Pardon?

ALEX. I'm married already. I have a wife.

LILY. *(Processing this.)* You already – Oh, I see. Oh, that's, that's – nice, then.

> *(A slight pause.)*
>
> *(Covering her embarrassment.)* I like your trousers, by the way. They're unusual.

ALEX. Oh, these? They're just my old jeans, terribly old. But seeing we were having this barbecue, I thought…

LILY. Jeans?

ALEX. Jeans. Originally from America.

LILY. *(Savouring the word.)* Jeans. Right. I must remember them.

ALEX. They'll be here soon enough. I like yours. Lovely colour.

LILY. Oh, heavens! Thank you for reminding me. I must change before we go round to Reg and Maude's. Reg doesn't approve of me wearing trousers. He never likes women in trousers. I came to work one day in a pair of slacks, he took one look and sent me straight back home to change. "Not having that in my shop, you come back when you're dressed properly, girl!"

ALEX. What did you do at Tindle's, then? Work behind the counter, did you?

LILY. Oh, no, not really, I didn't do much of that. All those hinges and one inch sevens. I couldn't cope with that. The lads did all that. I was mostly on the cash register. Then I did the cashing up in the evenings… I did the books, you know. For Mr Tindle.

ALEX. Oh, right. We're both in the same sort of line then…

LILY. Is that what you do? You a book keeper, are you?

ALEX. In a manner of speaking, yes. Did you enjoy it?

LILY. What, book keeping? No, I hated it. I could never get it to come out right, you know, balance. When I was adding up, I used to run out of fingers, you know. Alfie used to say, "take your shoes off then, Lil, use your toes as well." Mr Tindle, he used to stand over me some nights and he'd say, "we may be only a penny out, Lily, but it's that single penny that's going to bankrupt us in the end. Now, you check it again, young lady!" Some nights I was there till practically midnight, checking and re-checking… *(Examining a plate.)* Have you dried this? Only it's still wet.

ALEX. *(Taking back the plate, with a sigh.)* I still don't know why we're not using our machine next door. There's a perfectly good dishwasher there.

LILY. I told you, it's hardly worth it, is it? Great big machine, just for one or two odds and ends, quicker to do it yourself. I could never work in that kitchen it'd make me nervous. I mean it's all right for Rob. Good luck to him, if he's happy cooking in there, whipping up a soufflé…

ALEX. *(Somewhat mystified.)* Sorry? What?

LILY. You know, whipping up a cheese soufflé, like he does…

ALEX. Rob? *(She shakes her head in disbelief.)* I don't think so. I seem to remember, he did play a chef once, in an episode of *Poirot*, but I can't recall him ever… Whipping up a soufflé?

LILY. *(Smiling.)* Well. You never know what to believe with Rob half the time, really, do you?

ALEX. You've noticed that, have you? Lily, I think I should say a little about my brother... *(Proceeding with difficulty.)* He's – well, he's an actor, of course – and I must say on the whole, he's been a very successful one – until recently, at least – ups and downs of course, like most actors – but playing all these different people, as he does – it's not surprising he gets confused now and then. I sometimes wonder if he even knows who his real self is, half the time – he lives in a world where reality does tend to get a trifle blurred round the edges, if you follow me...

LILY. He lives in a world of his own?

ALEX. Precisely.

LILY. My brother was like that. He wasn't an actor. He went into plumbing eventually. But William was just like that when he was little. Making up things, you know. Pretending to be someone he wasn't. Inventing different names for himself. But he soon grew out of it, once he got apprenticed...

ALEX. Yes. The thing is, Rob never did quite grow out of it, you see. His apprenticeship was spent at RADA. Which probably aggravated matters. As a brother and sister, we couldn't be more different, if we tried.

LILY. You were saying, you're a book keeper, are you?

ALEX. In a manner of speaking, yes.

LILY. Lot of checking for you then, is there?

ALEX. Yes, I do have to make the – occasional check. To make sure we're not seriously over budget somewhere.

LILY. Where is it you work, then?

ALEX. I – I work in the – in the... I'm just a civil servant, really. I work for the government.

LILY. Oh, well. I'm impressed. I bet your boss doesn't breathe down your neck, does he?

ALEX. Oh, yes, she does. Quite frequently. No change in the workplace there, I'm afraid.

> *(Another triumphant yell from the garden as the football rolls into view, pursued by **ALF**.)*

ALF. *(As he enters, calling.)* Five nil to West Ham.

> *(He gathers up the ball and runs off again.)*

LILY. Hark at them! I'm pleased they both made it up, anyway! Mind you, he's like that, Alfie. He's sometimes quick tempered but he's over it just as fast. He's very forgiving. Never bears a grudge, not for long. I mean, once he'd punched him, once he'd knocked Rob out, that was it. All over, forgotten. Once we'd sorted out the misunderstanding. Realised he wasn't dead, after all.

ALEX. Who wasn't dead? Rob?

LILY. No, Alfie wasn't dead. I thought he was dead. That's why I fainted. I thought I'd seen a ghost.

ALEX. Why on earth did you think he was dead? What made you think that?

LILY. Rob told me. He told me Alfie was definitely killed in 1942. He must have got it wrong, mustn't he? Odd that.

ALEX. Yes. Very odd. He does occasionally get things wrong. Or he makes them up. He's – you probably noticed – he's very inventive.

LILY. I'd noticed. Told me he was a fireman originally. Tiger Jennings.

> *(**ALEX** hesitates. She is evidently, for her, in a very uncertain state.)*

ALEX. You know, I thought for one glorious moment he'd made all this up, too. The point is, Lily, I'm having a great deal of trouble accepting all this myself.

LILY. Accepting what?

ALEX. All of this. You. Your husband. The fact that I'm standing here, apparently in 1942 and outside it's pouring with rain. Whereas in our garden, next door, the sun's beating down, it's seventy-eight years ahead and we're well into the next century. And I've only to step through that hedge and I – I've this awful feeling I've actually stepped into one of my brother's make-believe worlds – I've wandered into one of his dreams. And in a minute, I'll suddenly wake up. Or maybe he'll suddenly wake up? Because this can't possibly be my dream, I never have dreams like this. Never. So here I am in this topsy-turvy, Wonderland world, waiting for him to wake up and make it all disappear. Put everything back as it was. Because, frankly, at heart, I'm a practical, down-to-earth person, Lily. In my job, I deal with concrete reality. Finite numbers. Hard facts and figures. Yes, I admit, like everyone, I sometimes take a wrong step, now and then, but nonetheless my feet always remain firmly on the ground. But now I have this feeling I'm floating six-foot in the air. With no visible means of support. And it's most terribly disconcerting, I have to say.

LILY. Glad he was wrong about Alfie, anyway. *(Awkwardly.)* By the way, I didn't – I didn't mention anything about this, all this to Alfie – about the different times – you and your brother being from a different time you know.

ALEX. No, very sensible.

LILY. I think it might be too much for Alfie to take in, what with everything else – with his mind being on the war, you know. You need to take care of them, don't you? I know he seems calm enough. Normally. But I know him. It's all going on in his head, you know. The fighting and that. Last night, after we – after we'd finished – you know – in bed. I fell asleep like I usually do. Only I woke up all of a sudden and he was lying there beside me, crying. Ever so quietly. I've never seen

Alfie cry before – *(Smiling.)* – well, perhaps on our wedding day but he did his best to hide it. Not manly to do that, is it? Crying? That's for girls. But I think it's better he doesn't know. I don't think he could take it in. Not at the moment. I'd appreciate it if you and your brother don't mention anything to him.

ALEX. No, we've already talked about that. We agreed. How about you? Don't you find it all disturbing? Personally? You seem so calm.

LILY. Well, no. I'm not really. I agree with you it's very odd. Extremely odd. But, you know, in the end, I look at it this way. It's just another thing for you to cope with, isn't it? I mean a couple of years ago, we were all happily living in this house, our first home together, we weren't that well off, but we were managing. And I could see the future clearly. And the next minute, it's all gone. My husband's suddenly sent away, risking his life in a war somewhere which I don't really understand anything about, my kids have been packed off somewhere else, only no one tells me where they are either, and all of a sudden, some foreigner I've never even met is dropping bombs on me. I think, if I'm honest, there's just been too much happening to me, too quickly. I can't quite take it all in. My brain – it's probably too small – it can't – deal with it all. So when someone steps through my hedge and tells me he's from the future, so what? It's just another thing to cope with, isn't it?

*(**ALEX** is somewhat moved by this. She holds out her arms. **LILY** moves to her and instinctively hugs her. **ALEX** responds.)*

*(A brief pause and then **LILY**, embarrassed, pushes herself away.)*

Sorry, I didn't mean to – I'm sorry.

ALEX. *(Somewhat amused.)* It's OK, Lily, you're quite safe. I'm a happily married woman.

LILY. *(Covering up the confusion.)* Yes. I think we're just about done in here, aren't we? Listen, I need to go upstairs and change. We're due round there to see his parents, Reg and Maude, his sister Margaret, if she's there – she's an ambulance driver, so she probably won't be – but Alfie's promised to see them, before he goes back. He needs to see his mum and dad, of course...

ALEX. Oh, yes, he must...

LILY. I'd offer you our facilities, only...

ALEX. ...only I'd never find the door, would I? Quite. Don't worry, if I need to, I'll go next door.

LILY. Probably better off there. Ours is a bugger to flush, like bellringing practice... takes ages...

ALEX. Maybe your brother could look at it...

LILY. William? Some hope. You can never get hold of him, he's that busy... won't be a second.

*(**LILY** goes.)*

*(**ALEX** watches her. Shakes her head, disbelievingly. She moves to the wall which she has seen **LILY** apparently walk clean through. She pats the space with her hands. It seems solid to her.)*

ALEX. *(To herself.)* Someone, help me please, I think I've fallen down a rabbit hole...

(She surveys the completed washing-up.)

*(She picks up the dishcloth and does a token wipe of the sink. But it is only cursory. **LILY** has apparently left things immaculate.)*

(She looks out of the window.)

Oh, well. Brave the rain, I suppose...

(She lets herself out of the back door and, taking a deep breath, she makes a quick dash as far as the gap in the fence and then through it and into the sunshine.)

Ah! Turned out nice again.

*(**ALF** enters bouncing the football. He is only mildly out of breath.)*

ALF. *(As he enters, triumphantly.)* West Ham nine – Portsmouth nil. How about that then? Walkover.

ALEX. Have you finished?

ALF. That's it! Full-time! Unless Portsmouth wants a replay...

*(**ROB** enters looking shattered and exhausted from the unaccustomed exercise. He clutches his side. He also has, as a result of yesterday, a black eye. He carries a summer cap.)*

*(To **ROB**.)* Fancy a replay, do you, Portsmouth?

ROB. *(Breathless, collapsing into a chair.)* Christ! I must start going to the gym again, I really must...

ALF. Here. *(He takes another can from the container.)* Get that down you!

*(He tosses the can to **ROB** and then helps himself to one.)*

ALEX. I thought you were supposed to be going round to see your family. Lily's just getting changed.

ALF. Oh, sure... In a minute. *(To **ROB**.)* Good, this beer. Not English, is it? *(Reading the can.)* Becks. Where's it come from, then?

ROB. – er...

ALEX. *(Interjecting swiftly.)* Kent.

ALF. Kent?

ROB. *(Blankly.)* Kent?

ALEX. Bexhill. Bexhill-on-sea.

ALF. Oh, right. Never knew that. *(To **ALEX**.)* How about you, darlin', you fancy a bit of Bexhill, do you? *(He winks at her.)*

ALEX. *(Smiling a little forcedly.)* No thank you, Alfie.

ALF. *(Looking over the hedge.)* Still raining that side, I see.

ROB. Oh, yes?

ALF. Peculiar that. I've never known rain, you know, cut off just like that. In a dead straight line. Straight along this hedge. Like two separate weather systems. Peculiar.

ROB. *(Stuck for a reply.)* Yes… It's…

ALEX. *(Likewise.)* Yes…

ALF. I'll tell you what I think is happening – I've been thinking about this, given it some thought…

ALEX. Really?

ROB. Oh, good…

ALF. I think what's happening is that all this bombing, all this German bombing, it's upset the usual weather patterns, you see…

ALEX. You think so?

ROB. That's an interesting theory…

ALF. …and it's disrupting the normal seasonal thermal currents, creating freak weather conditions, you see…

ALEX. Ah, yes of course, that would explain it…

ROB. Hadn't thought of that…

ALF. Blame the krauts for that as well then, eh?

ALEX. Absolutely.

ROB. Why not?

ALF. *(Cheerfully.)* Want to know something, ask me. Lily'll tell you. I'm forever putting her straight. Explaining things to her. *(Settling into a chair.)* No, with regards to the match, mate, you were let down by your goalie, that was your problem.

ROB. I was let down by my whole fucking team, that was my problem. The whole game was totally rigged, unfair from start to finish.

ALF. Same rules for both! Same rules applied.

ROB. Rubbish! You were making them up as you went along, half the time. Kept awarding yourself penalties every three minutes…

ALF. Well, there was a lot of very dodgy handball from your side…

ROB. That was when I was being my goalkeeper. I was allowed to handle it as my goalkeeper…

ALF. Yeah, but the rule was you had to put your cap on first. When you were being your goalie, you had to put your cap on, didn't you? That was the rule.

ROB. I notice you never put your bloody cap on. Never once.

ALF. Yeah, well, I never needed my goalie, did I? You never took a single shot, did you? I never needed mine.

ROB. Totally unfair!

ALF. *(To **ALEX**.)* Bad losers, eh, darling? *(He winks at her again.)*

ALEX. *(Who's had quite enough.)* Yes. If you'll excuse me, all this sporting talk, it's made this frail woman a little dizzy. I must go and freshen up.

ALF. Yes, you do that, darlin'. Powder your nose and all, eh? *(He winks at her again.)*

> *(ALEX draws a deep breath and moves to the kitchen door, grim faced.)*

(Watching her leave, to **ROB**.*)* Good looker, your sister, isn't she? She's got a great arse on her, too. For her age. Fancy her if she was younger.

ROB. I rather think you're barking up the wrong tree there, old boy. She's not really your type, if you follow me.

ALF. No, I said, she's too old.

ROB. What I meant was she's really not that interested in men.

ALF. What?

ROB. She's rather more attracted to women.

ALF. Oh, I see. *(He considers this.)* She's one of them, is she?

ROB. Yes. She's – one of them.

ALF. Ah. That's a problem. Has she been to see anyone about it?

> *(A silence as* **ROB** *has no reply.)*

(Shaking his head.) Glad Lil's not like that. Be a bit of a problem otherwise, wouldn't it, eh? *(He laughs.)* No, she's not that way. Not at all. She's – she's really something. You wouldn't guess it to look at her, not in daylight, but once she gets between the sheets, you know, she's something else again.

ROB. *(Uncomfortably.)* Oh, yes?

ALF. She's got an appetite on her – she's – vivacious – is that the word?

ROB. Voracious, I think…

ALF. Voracious, that's the one. I mean, last night – bloody hell, I thought the sodding bed was gonna go at one point. All over me, she was... You can't imagine...

ROB. *(Faintly.)* I think I probably can, yes.

ALF. I mean, I won't lie to you, I've had, you know, one or two girls over there, you know – professionals – nothing serious – but I have to say none of them was a patch on Lil... No, she's all right, the real thing is Lil.

(A slight pause.)

You got a wife, have you?

ROB. Yes, I – well two, I've had two. Only my second wife left me recently.

ALF. Oh, you lost her, did you? What was it? In an air raid?

ROB. No, no. She left me. She walked out. She married somebody else.

ALF. Oh, dear.

ROB. But I have a daughter, who's just started university. She's from my first wife. Who also left me.

ALF. She died then?

ROB. No, no. She's still alive as well. Very much alive and kicking – some other poor bloody soul, probably. She walked out, as well. But that was entirely my fault, that was.

ALF. Oh, yes? How come?

ROB. Let's say – youthful indiscretions, on my part...

ALF. Oh-ho-ho! Bit of a naughty boy, were you?

ROB. Just a bit. I was on tour in a play, you know, playing the lead. And there was this young juvenile, very attractive she was, probably only cast for her – attributes – rather than her acting talent, which was pretty negligible, poor kid.

*(Aware he now has **ALF**'s full attention, he warms to his story.)*

So, what the hell, I took pity on her, "Listen, darling, I can give you a few pointers, one or two little acting tips just to make our scene slightly better." Invited her back to my hotel. That's how it all started. By the time I got round to teaching her basic breath control, we were at it like a couple of randy rabbits…

ALF. Whey-hey! Bit of a lad in your day, then, weren't you?

ROB. *(Modestly.)* I had my moments…

ALF. How old were you?

ROB. About your age. Bit younger.

ALF. How did it finish?

ROB. Oh, some frustrated old bat from the wardrobe department, wrote to my wife. Tipped her off. All it took was one, spiteful anonymous letter…

ALF. What the hell did she do that for?

ROB. Well, you know women, especially women of that age. Probably wasn't getting any herself, that was her problem… I don't know. Maybe nursing a thing for me, I don't know… couldn't keep them away in those days, you know what it's like… *(He winces from a sharp pain in his head.)*

ALF. How's your eye? Any better?

ROB. Oh, yes, it's fine. Still got this slight headache. Probably from banging my head when I hit the floor.

ALF. Sorry about that. No hard feelings. I mean it was ridiculous, in hindsight. It was just you know, reflex reaction. I saw a bloke and I saw her holding him and I jumped to the conclusion, you know…

ROB. Perfectly natural, you would…

ALF. I mean, seeing you in the daylight, Christ, you're old enough to be her dad, aren't you?

(**ROB** *gives a sickly smile.*)

Lil explained to me, she was only holding onto you cos she was upset.

ROB. Right.

ALF. I never did ask her though – we were in that much of a hurry to get down to it, you know – I never did ask what she was so upset about.

ROB. *(Vaguely.)* I think – probably she was upset – because of the war and everything… Rationing and air raids and – the children being away. Missing you. Not being able to see any of you, you know…

ALF. Oh, yes. She dotes on the kids. Dotes on them. Think she prefers them to me sometimes. *(He laughs.)*

(**ROB** *smiles.*)

(Continuing more seriously.) Listen, mate, while we're on our own – just between us – I'm grateful to you keeping an eye out for her, you know. Fact is, I worry about her, being stuck here on her own – I know she's got the family just round the corner, but if anything were to happen to her… you know what I'm talking about…?

ROB. Oh, yes.

ALF. … I mean. before if she was ever in trouble, she'd have had no one except that old biddy next door, you know…

ROB. Mrs Doggett?

ALF. …if Lil were in trouble…she'd have been worse than useless, would Elsie. Hardly get up her own stairs… But knowing you two, you and your sister, you're here next door to keep an eye on her…it's a reassurance…that's all I'm saying.

ROB. We'll – we'll do our best to keep an eye on her.

ALF. Thanks, mate. Much appreciated. God bless you. Sitting out there, day after day – all those flies and the heat…makes you realise how important she is to you. Know what I mean? It's just that, after this trip, if I don't get back, you know, if I'm…

ROB. Oh, don't talk like that…

ALF. …No, seriously…

ROB. …You'll be fine, you'll come back…

ALF. …No, no, I'm being serious. It could happen – I mean, none of us can see the future, can we? We can't just say, that's not gonna happen, because it might. Listen, when we were first posted, there was me and three good mates, the four of us, close as that. The four musketeers. Special, you know. Now three of us are gone. I was actually holding one of them as he… *(He shakes his head.)* Point is, I'm the sole survivor. Now, I'm not a betting man but calculating the odds… let's say, if I survive, I'll be one of the very lucky ones. The very lucky ones. But the fact is, at the end of the day, that's not what matters, is it…?

ROB. I think you'll find it is, you know –

ALF. No, no, no, let me finish – what's important, what matters, what really matters – is her. That Lily survives. My kids survive. That's what's important. That's what we're fighting for, after all, isn't it? For them. For a better world for them to live in and all that.

ROB. Dear God, I hope it is…

ALF. But I tell you, all that would have been for nothing, if something happened to… something ever happened to… something… *(He is suddenly overcome with emotion.)* sorry, mate…

ROB. *(Concerned.)* Alfie? You alright?

ALF. *(Struggling to control himself.)* Yes. Yes. Fine. *(Jabbing at his eyes.)* Sorry, mate. I keep getting these fucking nightmares, you know. Right in the middle of the day sometimes. When I dream I lose them… Everything, you know, piling up on you…terrible dreams… I suddenly lose them all…can't find them anywhere…no matter how hard I …

(He is openly crying now.)

(As he cries.) …sorry, mate…sorry… I'm so sorry… *(Hitting his knee in frustration.)* …shit! …sorry… I'm so sorry…sorry…sorry, mate…

ROB. *(Soothingly, under this.)* It's alright… Alfie… It's okay… You can cry… It's okay to cry… cry if you want…

ALF. *(Finally controlling himself.)* God, sorry. *(Drying his eyes.)* What's the matter with me? Do us a favour, don't mention this to her, will you?

ROB. I don't see why not, if you –

ALF. No, she can't see me like this, it'd upset her – she needs me to be strong for her. If I start falling apart, how's she –? Shit! Pull yourself together, Alfred! You great girlie! Be ashamed of yourself!

ROB. Nothing to be ashamed of, Alfie, crying occasionally. We all cry now and then. I cry quite a bit. I nearly cried just now at my pathetic goalkeeping efforts. Hardly a week goes by without me…

ALF. It's all right for you, you're an actor, aren't you? Men aren't supposed to cry, are they?

ROB. Well, I like to think of myself as a man, first and foremost. And only increasingly occasionally, these days, as an actor…

*(**LILY** comes out of her kitchen into the garden. She is now wearing a skirt and has*

done herself up a little. She is carrying an umbrella.)

LILY. *(Seeing them.)* Alfie, you ought to get –

ALF. *(Immediately brightening.)* Here she comes, my little treasure! Over here, darling!

LILY. Alfie, you ought to get changed, you know. We're going to be late, otherwise.

ALF. It's alright I'll go like this...

LILY. No, put your uniform on...

ALF. I'm not changing into all that, just for a cup of tea...

LILY. No, wear your uniform. You know how proud it makes your mum when you wear your uniform...

ALF. Alright, alright, I'll wear it. Anything for a quiet life...

LILY. Finished your game, have you?

ALF. Ages ago.

LILY. Who won, then?

ALF & ROB. Who do you think?

LILY. Yes, well, you should have done. You're a lot younger than Rob. He's practically old enough to be your father, isn't he? I brought the brolly, but it's stopped raining, anyway. It's odd, isn't it? Raining one side and not the other like that?

ALF. *(Authoritatively.)* Yeah, I was just saying, the explanation for that is, with all this bombing you've been having, it's upset the usual weather patterns. It's disrupted the normal thermal currents, you see...

LILY. Oh, right. Isn't that interesting?

ALF. ...that's my theory.

LILY. *(Clutching his hand.)* Brilliant. *(To* **ROB**.*)* He knows everything, this one. He's a genius. *(Dragging him* *away.)* Come on then, Mr Einstein, come and put your uniform on…

ALF. … I'm coming, I'm coming…

LILY. See you later, Rob. We won't be that late. We'll be back before dark, certainly. In case there's an air raid…

(They climb through the hedge.)

ALF. I'll tell you one thing, once we're in bed, my love, I'm not getting out again just for a bloody air raid, I tell you that…

LILY. *(Giggling.)* Oh, Alfie! Really! You're terrible, aren't you, just terrible…

(They both go into their kitchen, closing the door and cutting off their voices. They continue to banter silently as they exit to the house.)

*(**ROB**, left alone, after a moment rises. He winces as he feels the consequences of his recent football game. He slowly begins to clear things away, the folding chairs and table, the cooling chest, etc.)*

ROB. *(As he does so, to himself.)* I am. I'm getting old. So old, old, old…

*(In a moment, **ALEX** comes from their kitchen.)*

ALEX. Hang on, I'll give you a hand with that…

ROB. Thanks.

(She joins to help him.)

(Together, during the next, they clear everything off to the end of the garden.)

ALEX. *(As she does so.)* Have they gone?

ROB. They won't be long. They need to be back before dark, anyway, because of the blackout.

ALEX. Oh, God, yes of course. They have blackouts, we have lockdowns. I'm sort of relieved really. I mean, I'm fine with her, don't get me wrong, we get on terribly well. But I do find him a bit of an obstacle course, if you know what I mean. I just wish to God he'd stop winking at me. Every time I say anything, he winks.

ROB. I think he probably sees you as a nice bit of totty...

ALEX. If only he knew...

ROB. He does now. I told him.

ALEX. *(Mildly amused.)* You did? What did he make of that, I wonder?

ROB. He asked if you were seeing anyone about it.

ALEX. *(Grimly.)* Well, I'm glad I wasn't here for that. War hero or not, he'd have finished up with a barbecue skewer up his arse.

ROB. I avoided race relations, anyway, just to be on the safe side. He's not a bad bloke, he's actually really rather nice. It's just he's – he's of his time, that's all.

ALEX. As are we, darling, as are we. You realise, in years to come – assuming, at the rate we're going, there are many more to come – they'll be saying that about us. You'll have to forgive them, dear, it's just they're of their time.

> *(They have now cleared the garden. All that remains are a few unopened cans of beer.)*

Is that it, then?

ROB. Better lock the shed. Deter barbecue thieves.

> *(He goes back briefly to lock up.)*
>
> *(She waits.)*

ALEX. Lily and I were saying just now, it's odd you got that date wrong. The date Alfie was supposed to have died. Everything else was right, except that.

ROB. *(Seriously.)* It's just possible – theoretically possible – that there are these so-called alternative timelines. Different futures if you like. Any one of which, depending on our course of action, we are able to follow…

ALEX. *(Intrigued.)* That's interesting. Where did you read that?

ROB. Oh, some pilot I did. For Netflix, I think. Ages ago. Forget the title.

ALEX. *(Losing interest.)* Oh, I see. More sci-fi.

ROB. Played a dodgy Russian diplomat, so far as I can remember. They scrapped it after season one.

ALEX. You mind if we go inside, it's getting a bit chilly?

ROB. Sure. *(Gathering up the cans of beer.)* I'll stick these remaining Bexhills back in the fridge. Bexhill-on-sea! What were you thinking of?

ALEX. It was the first place that came to mind…

ROB. You could have said Bexleyheath, at least it's in Kent…

(They move indoors.)

ALEX. *(As they enter.)* Thank God, we stopped Alfie coming in here. If he'd seen all this, he'd certainly have started asking questions, wouldn't he? A bit too macho though, isn't he, to venture into a kitchen…

ROB. *(Starting to put the beer away.)* I think he may have other problems than worrying about our kitchen.

ALEX. How do you mean?

ROB. I think he's got – how do you put it? – intimations of mortality. He believes his chances of survival are fairly slim, poor bloke.

ALEX. Oh, God, that's awful! How terrible...

ROB. *(Helping himself to beer.)* He asked me to – he asked us to – take care of Lily, if something happened to him. Look out for her and the kids, you know...

ALEX. What about his family? Can't they rally round?

ROB. I think he believes they're all a bit past it, you know...

ALEX. Well, we're hardly in the first flush of youth ourselves, are we? Either of us? I mean, <u>kids</u>? We couldn't possibly cope with kids, could we? Not at our age. What? Become glorified grandparents? I've avoided kids all my life, Rob, I can't be doing with them now, it'd be a total nightmare...

ROB. *(Trying to calm her.)* Yes, okay, okay. I only made a sort of half promise, that's all...

ALEX. ...Lily's a sweet girl and I do feel very sorry for her in her current situation, it must be hell on earth for her, but I mean, to be fair, I do have my own responsibilities, you know...

ROB. Yes, sure, I appreciate that...

ALEX. I mean, you're perfectly free at present, you can afford to make these promises, can't you...?

ROB. I wish I hadn't started this, you know...

ALEX. ...but to make a commitment like that, without even consulting me...

ROB. It was simply a verbal agreement between two blokes, that's all it was. Keep an eye on the missus while I'm away, would you? Yes of course. That's all it consisted of.

ALEX. Yes, well, leave me out of it. I have quite enough to cope with, what with Janice in her current state. You keep an eye on Lily, by all means, you're welcome to. You'll probably enjoy it too, won't you?

ROB. I think I would. I think I'm – I think, if it comes down to it, I'm probably a little bit in love with her, you know…

(A brief shocked silence.)

(Rather sheepishly.) Sorry.

ALEX. *(Sinking her head in her hands.)* Oh, Rob… Not again. You know I had this dreadful feeling this was happening… this awful premonition. How old is she? Twenty-something?

ROB. *(Subdued.)* Twenty-four.

ALEX. *(Continuing calmly.)* Twenty-four. She's a married woman with two children – and how old are they?

ROB. One's six, one's seven.

ALEX. …She has a husband whom she's passionately in love with…

ROB. …Which appears to be mutual on both sides, yes, I know…

ALEX. …And how old are you?

ROB. *(Softly.)* Sixty…

ALEX. Louder.

ROB. *(Loudly.)* Sixty. I'm sixty! As everyone keeps fucking reminding me!

(A pause.)

(More quietly.) Inside, I'm only twenty-five, though.

ALEX. *(Slowly.)* Your whole life's been like this, hasn't it? Your whole life? It's always been the same. You walk out the front door, you fall in love with the nearest lamp post! Rob, how could you? After all – your catastrophic relationships, affair after affair, two car crash marriages...

ROB. Look, I'm not planning to do anything with her –

ALEX. You should be so bloody lucky she'd even let you! You're old enough to be her grandfather. And even if you did manage something with her, by some miracle, what do you think that boy's going to do to you this time, the minute he finds out? You'd end up on life support...

ROB. I know, I know, I know all that...

ALEX. ...Well, I'm not coming to visit you in hospital, I'll tell you that... the only consolation, the one consolation I had amidst all this miserable current crisis with this wretched virus... the one thing I kept telling myself was, well, at least it'll keep my wretched brother at a safe social distance from female temptation... only for you to end up falling in love with someone seventy-eight years away...

ROB. I can't help it, I worry for her, that's all. She seems so innocent and fresh and – vulnerable. I worry for her so much, that's all...

ALEX. She's tougher than you think, Rob. I promise you, darling, she's a survivor. If anyone can survive that – hell they're going through at present – she will. *(Placing her hand on his.)* Believe me, you mustn't worry too much about her. You really mustn't.

> *(Her mobile phone chimes as a text message comes through.)*

(Glancing at the screen.) Oh, it's Janice. Better take it.

> *(She moves away a little to read the message.)*

(As she reads.) ...oh...oh...oh, dear...that is a problem. *(She closes her screen.)*

ROB. Mother trouble again, is it?

ALEX. No. Nothing to do with that. When I was talking to Janice earlier, I was trying to explain it all to her, what was happening here, not in great detail of course but she was interested. And I told her about Alfie and the fact that, despite what you found out, he'd turned out to be very much alive after all. And she's been online just now and, yes, she confirms you were right, the battle of El Alamein did indeed end on 27th of July 1942 …

ROB. Yes, so I read…

ALEX. But there was in fact a second battle of El Alamein which started on the 23rd of October 1942 and didn't finish until the 11th of November.

ROB. Oh, God. I didn't read that far.

ALEX. When's he due to travel back?

ROB. He's on a 48-hour leave, so not till late tomorrow, probably.

ALEX. Good. There's still plenty of time, then.

ROB. Time for what?

ALEX. Time to warn him, not to go back. We have to stop him going back, don't we?

ROB. We can't do that, then he'll be guilty of desertion. He'll most likely be shot as a deserter…

ALEX. He can't possibly go back, can he?

ROB. Either he goes back, and risks being shot by the enemy or he refuses to go, and he'll almost certainly be shot by our lot. A touch of the Hobson's, isn't it?

ALEX. Well, that's his decision. After all, it's his life and he needs to make his own choice.

ROB. I thought the idea was not to tell him?

ALEX. Things are different now. Lily ought to tell him herself. I know her instinct is not to but now she has to. He needs to be told.

ROB. First, someone needs to explain it to Lily, don't they? About there being a second battle…?

ALEX. Well, that's down to you, that's your job, darling.

ROB. *(Shaking his head at the prospect.)* You don't feel she might consider me the boy who cried wolf, rather? I mean, there's no possibility there was a third battle?

ALEX. No, there were only the two. After the second one, Rommel packed it in apparently. What's the best course of action, do you think? They'll be back soon, it's already starting to get dark. What do we do? Tell them now and ruin their evening? Or wait till tomorrow morning and ruin their day?

ROB. I think the sooner the better. I'll go next door and wait for them. Try and intercept them.

ALEX. You'll need to be quick. Knowing those two, the minute they're through the front door, they'll go racing up to bed. Want me to come with you?

ROB. No, it's best if it's just me. I'll talk to Lily first, explain what's happened. Then leave it to them both to talk it over. Better get going then, hadn't I?

ALEX. If you miss them, you can always try again in the morning, can't you? Good luck.

ROB. Yes.

> (**ROB** *steps outside into his garden. It has grown dark enough now for the security lights to again snap on.*)

(Reacting.) Whoops! Here we go, then.

ALEX. *(Watching him from the doorway.)* Okay?

ROB. Fine so far. I seem to recall, it'll get pretty dark on that side of the hedge, though.

ALEX. I'll tell you what, I'll try and keep the lights on for you. I'll stand here and keep waving my arms, shall I?

ROB. *(As he makes his way.)* I don't think that'll do much good. Our light doesn't seem to travel beyond the hedge, for some reason. I must ask Alfie about that. I'm sure there's a thermal current or two to explain it… *(Stepping through the hedge.)* Here I go then…

> *(He steps through the hedge and is immediately in darkness as the security lights snap off. He gropes his way forward towards the darkened house.)*

> *(**ALEX** goes back into the kitchen and, shortly afterwards, goes off.)*

Can't see a bloody thing…

> *(He finally makes it to the kitchen door.)*

> *(He tries the handle. It is locked.)*

> *(He knocks on the door gently.)*

(Calling gently.) Lily! Alfie! Anyone home? Hello! *(To himself.)* No, not back yet. Certainly good and dark now. Should be home by now, surely? Ah, well. Better lurk out here and wait, I suppose. So long as he doesn't mistake me for a burglar and come out and punch me again…

> *(The air raid siren sounds once more, very loud in the still clear night.)*

(Starting nervously.) Oh, my God! Air raid siren. Now what? Keep calm, now… no need to panic. Stay here. Keep absolutely still… they won't have seen you… not here in the dark…

(An explosion, reasonably close, as a bomb explodes nearby.)

(Reacting.) Oh, dear Lord! They've seen me! They must have seen me!

(Another explosion, even closer this time.)

(Growing slightly delirious.) Please, God, I don't want to die! Please don't let me die! I'll do anything you want me to! I swear, I'll do anything, anything!

(A third explosion, louder still.)

(Yelling over the din.) Forgive me for all the terrible things I've done! Forgive me my trespasses... *(Sudden inspiration.)* Air raid shelter! Of course, the Anderson shelter!

(As he starts to run down the garden towards the shelter, a triple explosion as three bombs fall close by in rapid succession.)

(As he flees.) Our Father which art in heaven, hallowed be thy name, thy kingdom come, thy will be done on earth as it is in heaven...

(His voice is drowned out as he goes off. Then the loudest explosion of all as number 17 takes a direct hit.)

(In the darkness, the terrible sounds of falling debris as the house is reduced to rubble.)

(A pause.)

*(**ROB**, having emerged from the shelter, enters cautiously. He now carries the shelter's emergency torch.)*

(Calling softly.) Lily? Lily? Alfie? Anyone there? Are you both all right? It's so damn dark, I can't see

a – *(Fiddling with the torch.)* Does this thing work at all...? Ah!

(The torch suddenly comes on.)

*(**ROB** scans the immediate area with the beam, gradually widening his area of search towards the house. It eventually falls across the first signs of brick rubble, the sad remains of all that is left of the house.)*

(With a soft cry.) No!

(He gradually explores the wreckage with the torch beam.)

(As more is revealed.) No, no, no, no, no, no, no...

VOICE. *(Loudly cutting through the night.)* Put that light out!

(The torch is immediately snapped out.)

(The blackout is total.)

End of Scene One

Scene Two

(The same.)

(Early the following morning.)

(The sun is already shining in both gardens.)

(The time for both houses is present day.)

(At number 17, the kitchen is now, in many respects, identical to its neighbour's, though how much we need actually see of this is a matter of choice.)

(In the garden, the vegetable patch has been replaced by a more conventional lawn and herbaceous borders.)

(At number 15, things look much the same. **ALEX** *sits in her dressing gown at the table, jabbing rather disconsolately at the keyboard of her laptop. She seems drawn and subdued having clearly spent the best part of the night crying.)*

(Also lying on the kitchen table is a large white unopened envelope, addressed to **ROBERT HATHAWAY** *which has been hand-delivered.)*

(In a moment, **ROB** *enters from the hall. He is also in his dressing gown and, like his sister, has clearly had an equally bad night.)*

ROB. *(Flatly.)* Hi.

ALEX. Hi. Did you sleep?

ROB. No. Did you?

(She shakes her head.)

(He moves to the window.)

ALEX. It all appears to be back as it was before. Next door. It looks very much as it used to do.

ROB. *(Studying it.)* Yes.

ALEX. *(In an attempt at humour.)* I'm sure the Jessops will be relieved, anyway.

ROB. I was lying there thinking just now, there's just the possibility that they both didn't make it home last night. That they stayed over with his parents. That they weren't next door when it happened.

ALEX. I've just been trawling the Internet trying to find some reference to her either surviving or dying but so far I haven't found anything. Plenty about Alfie, of course, the local hero and all that. Killed in action September 1942, El Alamein. So if he survived last night, then there's every chance that she would have done as well, isn't there? As far as we know, they could both be currently still alive and spending the day at his parents.

ROB. There's no way we can contact them anyway, is there? It's impossible to get to them now. The bombing last night – it obviously closed the – whatever it was – the portal. Can't reach them now, can we?

ALEX. Well, let's look on the bright side, shall we? Maybe they didn't come home last night, maybe they did stay over with his parents and maybe they all woke up safe and sound…?

ROB. …And he travels back this evening to North Africa and, in a month or so, he gets killed in action, without ever seeing his kids again, leaving her a widow and breaking her bloody heart. Looking on the bright side.

(A silence.)

(He sits at the table and slumps, very depressed.)

ALEX. I'm afraid it's sausages again this evening. Can you bear to have them again?

ROB. I don't mind.

ALEX. Unless you feel like whipping us up a soufflé?

ROB. *(Noting the envelope for the first time.)* What's this, then?

ALEX. No idea. It came through the door first thing. By hand.

ROB. Who's it from?

ALEX. I've no idea. I haven't opened it, it's addressed to you.

ROB. More misguided fan mail. From deluded old-age pensioners. No, I can't be bothered. Chuck it in the bin.

ALEX. No, Rob! Don't be so churlish and ungrateful. If someone has taken the trouble to write to you, the least you can do is have the courtesy to read their letter.

ROB. *(Tossing the envelope to her.)* Here, you read it.

*(**ALEX** sighs and opens the large envelope. Inside is a slip of paper on which is written a brief note and also a smaller pink envelope, addressed to **ROBERT HATHAWAY**. She lays the pink envelope to one side and studies the note.)*

ALEX. Hmm! Well. You may be right… *(Reading.)* Dear Mr Hathaway, my late mother who died a few years ago aged ninety-four was, throughout her life, a devoted fan and wanted me to pass on the enclosed letter. She was, towards the end, somewhat wayward in her thinking but nonetheless was insistent that I wait until today, the seventh of August, to deliver this to you at the earliest opportunity. I have done my best to comply with her wishes and trust this reaches you safely. Yours sincerely, Constance Harper, brackets Mrs.

ROB. What the hell's that all about, then?

ALEX. Very odd.

ROB. Dear God, they're getting dottier and dottier, aren't they, the older I get? It's bad enough getting letters from ninety-four-year-olds but now I'm getting letters from fans from the cemetery! God, this is so depressing. *(Rising.)* I can't cope, I can't cope any more... *(He paces the room.)*

ALEX. *(Slightly impatiently.)* Oh, come along, darling, read her mother's letter. You can at least acknowledge you received it...

ROB. *(Angrily.)* What's the point of acknowledging it? The woman's dead and buried, for Christ sake...?

ALEX. You can at least write to this Mrs – whatever her name is – Mrs Harper to say you were very touched by her mother's letter and you greatly sympathise with her loss, et cetera et cetera...

ROB. Yes, that's great! Great! You write it then! You write the bloody thing...

ALEX. *(Slapping the table irritably.)* Rob, will you sit down at once and pull yourself together! You're behaving like a spoilt child! Sit down, do you hear! Sit!

(**ROB** *sits sulkily.*)

(Continuing more calmly.) Now I'm going to open this letter and I'm going to read it to you. You don't have to read it yourself but I refuse to write the reply for you. You're going to have to do that yourself, do you hear?

(**ROB** *is silent.*)

(Opening the letter.) Right. Are you listening?

ROB. *(Gloomily.)* I made a promise, you know. I made Alfie a promise I'd look after her if he – wasn't there. I can't even manage that, can I? God, what a failure I am! An abject bloody failure...

ALEX. *(Calmly.)* Rob, kindly be quiet and allow me to read this to you, please...

ROB. ...Everything I touch, every relationship I have, I go and wreck it...every single one of them...

ALEX. ...I warn you, you're on the verge of wrecking another relationship, Rob, if you're not careful... Ready? Are you listening? *(Reading.)* Dear Robert Hathaway, or may I call you Rob? It seems so –

ROB. *(Interrupting fiercely.)* No, you certainly can't call me Rob, madam!

ALEX. Rob!

ROB. Bloody cheek! No. I'm sick to death of it, these days, everyone wants to be on first name terms, every Tom, Dick and carpet salesman – *(Staring at the letter in her hand.)* Hang on! I know that pink paper...that writing, that lurid purple ink... it's identical to the one in the downstairs loo... that letter I had framed...

ALEX. My God, so it is.

ROB. ...The one I stare at every single morning, whenever I take a piss. It's the same woman! It has to be! She never even bothered to sign the other one. "A concerned fan", she called herself. How's she signed this one?

(**ALEX** *turns the page over.*)

ALEX. *(After a slight pause.)* Lily.

ROB. *(Hoarsely.)* Lily?

ALEX. Brackets Tindle. Can't get clearer than that, can you?

ROB. *(Taking it all in.)* She survived? She did survive, then?

ALEX. Until she was ninety-four, apparently. Pretty good going.

ROB. And the woman who brought the letter round this morning...?

ALEX. Constance Harper. Brackets Mrs.

ROB. Was Connie. Her daughter. What's she say in her letter? Read it.

> *(**ALEX** starts to scan the letter briefly. **ROB** waits.)*

ALEX. *(Finally shaking her head, a trifle moved.)* Oh, no, this is all too personal, you need to read it yourself, Rob.

> *(She rises.)*

(Placing the letter in front of him.) Here, I'll leave it with you. I think you two need to be alone, I really do. I'll be upstairs...

> *(She moves to the door, hesitates, and turns.)*

(Smiling.) There's a rather amusing bit, I have to tell you. Remember that tour you did in the early days? The one when you were bonking your fellow juvenile? The one that finally broke up your first marriage?

ROB. The tour of *Not in These Trousers*, yes. Will I ever forget it?

ALEX. Apparently, Lily got a job as a wardrobe assistant just to be near you. She's the one who blew the whistle on you, darling.

ROB. *(Incredulous.)* That was – that was <u>her</u>? I would never have – she was – she was so –

ALEX. – so old, you're going to say? Well, she must have been in her mid-sixties by then. And you were what? – still in your 20s, weren't you? So perhaps old to you. You probably didn't even give her a second glance. It never works both ways, does it? I tell you, it's still a tough world for us women. Do read it, Rob, won't you? She stuck with you through it all. The least you can do is to thank her.

>*(She goes out.)*
>
>*(**ROB** sits silently for a moment.)*
>
>*(He picks up the letter and starts to read it.)*
>
>*(His reaction changes from amusement to amazement and finally tears, as revelation after revelation unfolds.)*
>
>*(He gently lays the letter down.)*

ROB. *(At last, softly tearful.)* Thank you, my darling, thank you.

>*(Music starts* under and, as it builds, the lights fade to a: –)*
>
>*(Blackout.)*

End of Play

---

* A license to produce *The Girl Next Door* does not include a performance license for any third-party or copyrighted music. Licensees should create an original composition or use music in the public domain. For further information, please see the Music and Third-Party Materials Use Note on page iii.

www.ingramcontent.com/pod-product-compliance
Ingram Content Group UK Ltd.
Pitfield, Milton Keynes, MK11 3LW, UK
UKHW021840210426
5322IPUK00022B/381